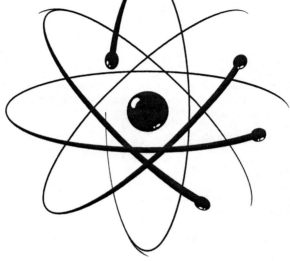

RadioActive Leadership

Roy E. Alston

First published by AuthorHouse 05/12/05

ISBN: 1-4208-5096-2 (sc)

Printed in the United States of America
Bloomington, Indiana

This book is printed on acid-free paper.

Table of Contents

Introduction

"In every phenomenon the beginning remains always the most notable moment"

- Thomas Carlyle

Welcome to RadioActive Leadership.

This is a book for people in the front lines of business and life - for people who've learned more from practical experience than they have from formal education. We don't care if you don't have an MBA or advanced degree; this book isn't written for CEOs, CFOs or for the CIA. It's a practical, tactical guide for everyone on the firing line of business: sales, customer service, medical and educational practices, municipal services, law enforcement, legal services, and much more.

If you're reading this book, it's possible you've never had formal "leadership" training - if that's the case, it's a bonus for you. In an odd twist, most leadership books are written for people who are already leaders, or training to soon be one. While many of those people will benefit from this book, it's not written specifically for them. This book is written for you - the regular guy on the front lines, the leader by default or the guy who most people turn to, to get direction or answers. You know who you are.

You're educated but maybe not as much as you'd like. You've learned many of your skills and acquired much of your knowledge from the work itself - you learn by doing, not by talking about it. You know your craft; you're good at what you do.

You've already been thrown into situations where, out of necessity, you are required to lead, to take over a project or task, to form a team or group, to solve yesterday's problem that was supposed to be solved last week. You've already had to bail out a faulty mission, fix a flawed process and make a sale that was already lost. You're not exactly sure how you did it, but against overwhelming odds, you did it anyway. And after it was done and a big hit, virtually nobody remembered that you were the one who got it done. Welcome to the real world of business.

In order to get it done, you instinctively did some of the right things: you got some ideas from a close group of associates, you worked out a plan of action, you uncovered pitfalls and obstacles; you planned your way toward success. You opened communication around the group; you worked hard to achieve the impossible. And, a few times, you got really lucky. In short, you took over - you became a leader without ever really knowing that was what you were supposed to do.

This book is for you. To confirm many of the things you instinctively know about leading people; to share new ideas and refine your already-solid abilities. This book will also give you no-nonsense suggestions on leadership, team management, motivation, discipline, personal development, idea generation and a lot more.

We're not going to get fancy on you - not a lot of MBA language or exotic philosophy. We're not going to bore you with a million statistics, flow charts and behavioral matrices. We'll get into your head a little, and the heads and hearts of the people you work with, but we won't overdo the Freudian analysis. (Freud was an okay leader, but he could also be a painful bore.) And mostly, we're not going to snow you with the "secrets" of leadership. Leading people takes hard work - to do it right, you've got to show up early and stay late. You've got to learn and teach at the same time. You've got to be tough enough to get the job done and nice enough so that people want to work with you again and again. You've got to care about what you do - so much that it shows in every step you take, in every action and thought. Okay, it's not an easy job - but nobody ever told you your job would be easy, did they?

Our examples are people like you - they fought their way up from the front. Our lessons are realistic and uncommon sense - learned from real life situations. It's not fancy, but it's proven to be effective - ingrained and tested under extreme situations.

There are no "secrets" to leadership - there have been leaders since we came out of the caves. The lessons are there to be learned, to be lived. We've lived through many of the practical lessons, drawn from military training and practice, law enforcement and the front lines of business training. We've seen a great deal of the front lines of the business world - and we're going to share what we've learned.

We're going to walk you through a step-by-step process to make sure you will not only understand the lessons but also be able to apply them immediately.

We're here for you. We've got a website - www.radioactiveleadership.com: we'll answer every question you've ever had - or ever will have. Let's get started.

RadioActivity

"A strong, successful man is not the victim of his environment. He creates favorable conditions. His inherent force and energy compel things to turn as he desires."

- Orison Swett Martin

Radiation is defined as "energy emitted in the form of particles." RadioActive Leadership is energy offered to the people around you - to stimulate, challenge, encourage, direct and support them. RadioActive Leadership is inside and outside, up and down and left and right. Another way of looking at RA Leadership is:

* Self-leadership = inside and outside
* Leadership that can impact peers = left and right
* Leadership for those who work for you and those you work for = up and down

The sun radiates heat - a bulb radiates light - jokes radiate laughter - good ideas radiate action - radiators keep the house warm and RA Leaders do all these things and more. RA Leaders both attract and promote the people around them; they provide energy and direction, enthusiasm and expertise. An RA Leader is that great teacher you had in school - the one who made the subject fun and exciting. An RA Leader is that coach who got you to play better than you ever had played.

It's up to you now. By using some common sense, employing basic leading skills and putting yourself out there - you not only can lead other people, you must lead other people. Leadership is not just a talent or ability; it's also a responsibility. Those who can lead must lead - because not everyone can take charge. There are many people who prefer to remain unseen and unheard. As you've been told all your life - you're not one of those folks.

You've got the qualities of leadership - the only thing you lack is the knowledge. We'll supply that information to you. This is your journey, are you ready?

The Laws of RadioActive Leadership

"A leader has the vision and conviction that a dream can be achieved. He inspires the powers and energy to get it done."

- Ralph Lauren

RadioActive Attraction

The first law of RA Leadership is to maximize your value to yourself and everyone around you. The more knowledge, expertise, ability, mastery and comprehension you possess, the more valuable you become to everyone around you. This is your attraction.

RadioActive Responsibility

The second law of RA leadership is the fact that RadioActivity is a powerful attribute - it positively affects everyone that it comes into contact with and it moves everyone to excellence. This is your responsibility.

So, how does this work? Good question. Let's take an example of a team action you may have to fulfill (think about this seriously for a couple of moments, as we are about to drill down just a little to begin thinking in slightly different terms). As we work down through our checklist, answer all the questions and draw your own mental link to the two rules:

Are you willing to risk?

It's very likely that no one has told you to go out and build this team. The people above you may not even see the problems that are common in the everyday experiences of you and your group. *It's up to you to get the group together - to get to work on the opportunities or problems right in front of you.*

Are you willing to build a functional team?

Can you find the people you need? They're all around you, but you have to go get them. Talk to your peers - find out if they're facing the same problems and dealing with similar hurdles that you confront. As soon as you open the dialogue, the leadership has begun. Remember though, it's important to focus on issues in order to develop actions and resolutions. Gripe sessions are not the same as brainstorming sessions.

Do you have enough group knowledge and expertise to execute the mission? As Thomas Edison said, "Genius is one percent inspiration and ninety-nine percent perspiration." You must be able and willing to do the grunt work to get the job done beyond even your own expectations.

Are you willing to develop a consensus?

Have you opened the planning process to everyone involved in the mission? (Of course you have the best ideas of anyone around... but you're also the team leader or a team member. Your job is to encourage everyone, to get the best out of each person in order to solve the problems you face or achieve the goals you desire.)

Are you getting solid responses from everyone? (Yes, you're allowed to have shy types in any team. But shyness is not sufficient reason not to participate. Build an environment where everyone is expected to participate by offering their ideas and analysis.)

Have you opened the process to those above, to the side and below you? (Great input comes from every direction - good ideas are not only passed down from above. Gather contributions from all directions.)

Are you willing to identify needs?

Do you know what you've got? You must know what sorts of resources, and how many resources, you've got to work with. Find out what levels of expertise your team mates possess. Explore options for knowledge you may need to acquire.

Do you know what you're after? Too many missions go astray simply because people aren't sure, or lose sight, of the target. Set achievable goals and expand from success.

Are you willing to plan?

Are you organized? Do you have the vision to know what's needed? As an RA Leader, you can't permit any excuses - for yourself or your team. Planning and preparation are difficult items - but as necessary as air. As Sun Tzu wrote more than 2000 years ago, "All battles are won BEFORE they are fought."

Are you willing to plan for the unplanned?

Can you lead during crisis? In every process, there are times of uncertainty, if not outright disaster. YOU are the one who must keep his or her head; YOU are the one who will set the tone for the rest of the group. You have to keep your wits when everyone is losing theirs.

Are you willing to take action?

Do you relish the activity? Are you addicted to the action? As an RA Leader, even the leaders above you will be affected by your emotional connection, your personal commitment to achieving your goals. It's not enough to just get the job done - you have to get it done with energy, enthusiasm and electricity. You are the power.

 Are you willing to be realistic?
Can you achieve your objectives? Have you set your sights accurately? Team morale is dependent on the ability to achieve the tasks necessary to attain the ultimate goal - people work harder if they know they can win. Especially in the formation and initial operations of a team, practice short-term targets that have high probability of success. Good teams concentrate on fundamentals that bring success in the short and long term.

Are you willing to measure effectiveness?
Can you tell if you've made a difference? Can you show your accomplishments? At some

point in the game, everyone wants to know the score - it's the final proof that you've won the contest. Create criteria that are identifiable, clear and accurately demonstrates the rewards of your actions. At some point, the team will look directly to you - to show the world their success. Be ready to show it.

Are you willing to offer rewards and provide recognition?

What do you get when it works? What does the team get? Many times, a pat on the back is the best you can expect. And just as many times, you won't even get that much recognition. IT'S UP TO YOU to provide the recognition of a job well done. Sometimes that's as small as a thank you note or a bag of bagels; sometimes it's letters of commendation to superiors. Sometimes it's much more. Whatever it is, plan for rewards and recognition with the same attention you pay to planning and execution.

Allow me a brief digression:

If there is one factor missing from team-building today, it is the inability of managers to recognize good effort, solid work and worthy results. This lack of acknowledgment runs through entire industries: retail sales, service sector, the private and public sectors

It's almost as if management considers blue-collar or front-line workers expendable enough to turn them out, rather than offer rewards for performance or encouragement for a job well done. This bizarre mentality causes the specific effect of turning over entire strata of industries:

Employee Turnover Rates: Voluntary by Industry (September 2003 - August 2004)

Total US	20.20
Private Industry	22.80
Natural Resources and Mining	16.10
Construction	25.40
Manufacturing	14
Durable Goods Manufacturing	13.70
Nondurable Goods Manufact.	14.80
Trade	24.90
Wholesale Trade	16.10
Retail Trade	31.20
Transportation	14.60
Information	14.90
Financial Activities	14.10
Finance and Insurance	12.20
Real Estate, Rental & Leasing	20.10
Professional & Business Services	21.40
Education and Health Services	17.10
Educational Services	9.8
Health Care & Social Assistance	18.40
Leisure and Hospitality	44.40
Accomodations & Food Services	26.80
Other Services	47.30
	24.40

Data is supplied by the U.S. Department of Labor.

19

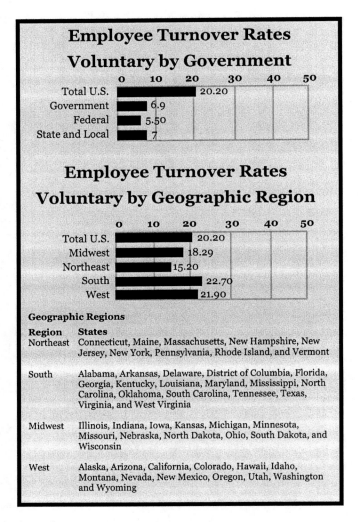

Employee Turnover Rates
Voluntary by Government

	0	10	20	30	40	50
Total U.S.			20.20			
Government	6.9					
Federal	5.50					
State and Local	7					

Employee Turnover Rates
Voluntary by Geographic Region

	0	10	20	30	40	50
Total U.S.			20.20			
Midwest			18.29			
Northeast		15.20				
South			22.70			
West			21.90			

Geographic Regions

Region	States
Northeast	Connecticut, Maine, Massachusetts, New Hampshire, New Jersey, New York, Pennsylvania, Rhode Island, and Vermont
South	Alabama, Arkansas, Delaware, District of Columbia, Florida, Georgia, Kentucky, Louisiana, Maryland, Mississippi, North Carolina, Oklahoma, South Carolina, Tennessee, Texas, Virginia, and West Virginia
Midwest	Illinois, Indiana, Iowa, Kansas, Michigan, Minnesota, Missouri, Nebraska, North Dakota, Ohio, South Dakota, and Wisconsin
West	Alaska, Arizona, California, Colorado, Hawaii, Idaho, Montana, Nevada, New Mexico, Oregon, Utah, Washington and Wyoming

Imagine the cost-savings in training, hiring and efficiency if current employees stayed in their positions longer. Imagine the vast increase in productivity and profits that a base of committed workers would gain. Estimates are virtually impossible to calculate. What is possible to estimate is the bottom-line effect on companies that fail to retain committed employees.

The table on the following page shows the potential savings per year for select companies if they were to reduce their employee turnover by just 1%. These figures are based on public data from *Fortune* Magazine's 100 Best Companies to work for, January 2001. The estimated turnover cost used below is based on 20% of the most common entry level salary of each company. This is a very conservative estimate. In reality, these costs can be much higher. HR professionals estimate this cost between 50% and 125% of an employee's salary. The recruiting commission alone can range between 20-30% of salary. Realized savings would thus tend to be significantly higher than illustrated below. Note that for just a one percent decrease in turnover, every company could realize a one year savings between 200 thousand and 2 million dollars.

Company[1]	Number of Employees (US)	Turnover Rate	Estimated Turnover Cost per employee[2]	Reducing Turnover 1% Savings / year
Merck	39,489	9%	$7592	$2,765,000
Cerner	2,953	14%	$8000	$240,000
Charles Schwab	18,863	12%	$8329	$1,512,000
MBNA America Bank	16,960	15%	$4800	$1,000,000
Av. US Company	10,000	15.6%	$5000	$500,000

Notes:
1. Based on Public Data from *Fortune* Magazine's 100 Best Companies to work for Jan. '01.
2. Estimated Turnover Costs calculated at 20% of most common entry level salary as provided in note 1.

A New Way

"The whole of science is nothing more than a refinement of everyday thinking."

- Albert Einstein

It has been said that creativity is the ability to create something out of nothing. True innovation begins with only the idea or the need for it; creativity doesn't depend on inspiration as much as necessity or urgency. RadioActive Leaders are curious by nature, creative and interested. They work on new ideas because that's where they find the greatest personal and professional rewards.

RA Leaders grow comfortable with creativity because they constantly practice it. They burn out the fear of risk or rejection because those judgments aren't relevant to the core process. RA Leaders intuitively understand that creativity is an ongoing, sometimes lifelong, process - not merely a tool to achieve one or two results. Creativity becomes a personal lifestyle, a calling and a talent that forms their future.

In the next areas, we're going to examine your world, the zones of your work-life, to identify and address areas where you can begin to make not just a difference, but also a change for the good. These charts are dedicated to your personal development.

Let's begin at the beginning. Make an active and conscious choice to become aware of the problems and obstacles around you. (As you already know, there are plenty of them around the business world. We spend most of our time either overcoming them or ignoring them.) Frustration is the difference between the life you are living and the one you actually want. As children, we didn't know what we wanted to be as grown-ups. As adults, we know what thrills us, but sometimes were too frightened to pursue those dreams.

In our new operations plan, we ignore no more - instead we dive in and get to work. Our next steps are Awareness/Identification,

Assessment, Action/Tools and Determination.

⚛ Awareness/Identification

Let's take a look at you. Are you where you want to be? Are you living and working to your full potential? Can you see room for improvement? List a few of the things that can use improvement. Remember to drill down deep, until all that remains is "you" and the issue at hand. Nothing else matters. Okay, list away:

_____

_____

_____

_____

_____

_____

_____

Assessment

Select one of the areas you've noted for improvement. It helps to make the first choices the easiest options to accomplish. Define the area of the problem as much as you can. Be analytical, literal and specific. What is the issue? Is it large or small? Does the problem repeat frequently? List areas that need work:

_____

_____

_____

_____

_____

_____

_____

_____

Action/Tools

Action - who can you talk to, to define areas of need? Where can you find information to address the issues? What resources can you find or apply?

Tools - what steps can you take to address areas that need improvement? (Skill training, primary/secondary/advanced education, "soft-skills" like public speaking, sales training, etc.)

List action steps you can take - also list the tools you'll need to accomplish the improvement:

Actions   *Tools*

_____

_____

_____

_____

_____

_____

Determination

Here's another concept you already know: plans are one thing; results are something else. Every person in the world would own their own country - if they just had the determination and persistence to actually do it.

We will enforce our own determination by creating contracts for ourselves - business agreements that we'll create and impose on our own behavior. We'll make promises that we will plan to keep. These aren't some pie-in-the-sky deals that we forget tomorrow - we're writing them down and we're going to check our progress every week.

Go to www.radioactiveleadership.com and download your personal development contract. Simply fill it in, save it to the website, and print. We will follow up on you by sending you a reminder and encouragement.

_____

_____

_____

Teaching People to Learn

"Minds are like parachutes - they only function when open."
— *Thomas Dewar*

This sounds like a strange concept, doesn't it? - teaching people to learn. It's simpler than you think and more unusual in business than you'd ever imagine. Training employees in the business world is devoted to task-orientation: providing basic information necessary to execute a specific function or purpose. Cashiers are trained to operate the register; factory workers are trained to run the assembly line; waiters are trained to explain the menu and take the orders. In mid- and upper-management, task-orientation is expanded - training is done in institutions of higher education and specialized expertise. But the concept is basically the same: CFOs learn to project and maintain a budget; managers learn to hire and supervise a staff; vice-presidents learn to take credit for everyone else's work. (I kid - but not by much.)

Throughout the various levels of training, people's learning is motivated by different factors:

People learn by incentive:
- the promise of a rewarding position or career
- the hope of advancement and opportunity
- the ultimate goal of safety, prosperity and security

People also learn through adversity:
- "Hey, we're losing money - this budget isn't working"
- "My last job imploded, now what?"
- "Customers aren't staying. What can we do?"

People learn through affinity and appeal:
- "I love to paint. I'll take some classes."

· "I'm pretty good with numbers."
· "I don't know what it is. I just have a knack for it, I guess."

First We Learn to Learn

RA Leaders not only become good teachers - their associates and teammates also become good students: people who enjoy the active process of learning. The old axiom: those who can't do, teach, might be a bad joke, but it's also a lie. Great teachers are also great students. They are people who, by choice and profession, love their subjects and love to share that passion with people around them. The best teachers have "been there and done that" - they know what you will need to get the job done. They have confidence in their expertise and mastery of their subject. The joy they express in sharing their skills with you defines the precise amount of pleasure you derive from the subject. Think about this idea for a moment: the teachers you enjoyed the most were those that demonstrated their joy for the subject - which made you want to learn more about it. It's almost that simple - great teachers love their craft and they love to share that passion with students. For great teachers, this is why they teach - the love of the craft.

This trait begins with you. The first law of Teaching People to Learn is to become an excellent student yourself - to learn to learn. Radio-Active Leaders are also RadioActive Learners - they cultivate a lifelong love of learning. For many people, embracing the idea of learning is a hard step to take - but it's a necessary trait to acquire. To put it bluntly, few people are going to have faith in a manager or peer who tells them to perform a function that the manager/peer can't or won't perform. You're not going to follow your platoon leader into battle if you're not sure he can fire his weapon. And weapons change every day - they get faster and more complex; they become harder to fix and understand. This is a law of the world around us.

You must learn to love to learn... (Sounds

like a song is about to start.) There are many traits that great students share, in order to open themselves to acquire knowledge and immerse themselves in the process of learning.

Traits of Great Students:

Admission

Being a great student means admitting you may not know everything - an admission that is incredibly difficult for many people to express in the business world.

Fanatical Desire

Great students must want to learn. Whatever trick or incentive you need to create, you must actually want to learn. Learn more skills for your next raise or to get a better job or to buy your dream home - it doesn't matter what your desire is, as long as your desire is high.

Vulnerability

Great students know they have a lot to learn. They don't care what other people think

- they're going to learn for their own purposes.

Risk
Great students have to take chances as they test new knowledge; trial and error is as old as mankind and great students have to be willing to try, and through trying, great students will sometimes fail.

Offer
Great students share their ideas and opinions in a positive, respectful way. They know the other students around them are just as vulnerable and hopeful as they. Great students speak up, offer ideas, challenge concepts, exchange information and much more.

Encourage
Great students encourage learning in those people around them. They support their peers by offering help and reassurance - they do this voluntarily and easily.

☢ Understand

Great students know the information they are acquiring, even if it doesn't appear immediately useful, will help them in the long run. They know that knowledge may not be instantly understandable or applicable - but they learn to enjoy the process in any event.

☢ Rewarding

Great students learn to reward themselves and their peers for the knowledge they've gained. Rewards can be as small as a pat on the back for mastering the workings of a new machine or as grand as suggesting a peer for promotion because of their mastery of a business process. Great students don't wait for acknowledgement from above - they create rewards and recognition by themselves. It doesn't matter if the reward is a piece of ribbon wrapped around a cookie - or a raise - RA Learners create their own reward system. RA Leaders reward those around them. They understand, and know how to trigger, the formal reward system of your organization. (You know, the one the company has on paper that no one knows how to work.)

When you immerse yourself in the learning process, discovering everything about a system or process - knowing all you can know about your area of expertise, you inspire those people around you to immerse themselves as well.

Learning to learn is a lifelong pursuit. In classical renaissance beliefs, philosophers held an interesting theory: the very function of life was to acquire knowledge and skill, to learn and discuss arts and sciences, to explore and investigate ideas and ideals. Some of the greatest discoveries, inventions and artistic expressions were developed directly from this notion. Theorists challenged "laws" of science, sculptors refined and perfected great works - even oceans were crossed and new worlds discovered in the pursuit of knowledge (and also the treasure that may come from discovery).

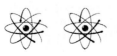

RadioActive Values

"Men of genius are admired. Men of wealth are envied. Men of power are feared. But only men of character are trusted."

- Alfred Adler

RA leaders are battlers by nature - you have to be. You're on the front lines, on the business edge - you don't have the luxury of a large office, a golden parachute or third chance. When you succeed, it may not be noticed; when you fail, look out below. You've been given just about nothing; everything you have you've earned through sweat and common sense. These traits make you street-smart and tough, tenacious and determined. These are important values for a RadioActive Leader but they're not the only ones you'll need to succeed.

Your core values - the principles on which your life is based - must be consistent, apparent and as firm a foundation as you can achieve. Because you won't get many third chances, you must live a life based on core values that will sustain you during challenges and inspire you during opportunities. You're one of the grunts, on the front lines - in order to advance up the ladder (or build your own ladder) - you can't afford lapses in character.

There's an important distinction here:

In business, errors in judgment are usually acceptable while lapses in character are more difficult to manage. For example, you may be able to stall a client with a white lie or two, but if you try the same fibs on the boss, you'll be out the door comparatively soon. Fortunately, there is a precise way to avoid the hazards of business life: live your life based on sound principles and superior core values.

RadioActive Leadership Value #1
Fanatical Listening

Has anyone ever offended you because

they carefully listened to you? Have you ever been insulted because someone cared deeply about what you were saying? Is it possible to listen too well? The answers to these questions are obvious - listening is one of the most powerful tools and skills a leader may have. And listening can make the difference between a good leader and a great one.

Hear What They Are Feeling

Listening is not simply hearing the words - it is also the ability to understand and build empathy with that person's needs. Listening is the first step to serving - and serving is the very purpose of leadership.

RadioActive Leadership Value #2
Truth in Business (and Life Too)

While it may seem obvious that Radio-Active Leaders must be truthful at all times - *you must also offer truth whenever possible.* Leaders must not only embrace candor as their prime operating mode, they must also take the responsibility to nurture and promote frankness in people around them. It's a simple principle: *great leaders must tell the truth and they must hear the truth - they must encourage truth-telling and accept both benefits and consequences of it.* If a team suspects they are being misled, there is no quicker way to lose them.

The agenda must be open and honest. You can't tell your team a new process or idea is good for them when the truth doesn't support it. Team members ALWAYS know the truth! Be transparent. Let your team see what you see and know what you know. You'll be surprised how quickly they see the benefits of a new process or program.

As important as it is to tell the truth, it's equally important to offer the truth. When project plans seem to be going astray, when your team moves in a questionable direction - your inclination may be to "go with the flow" or "leave it alone." In order to lead well, you must fight this tendency. State your concerns concisely, firmly and to the point - offer the value of your expertise to the group. If you don't understand the mission, tactics or strategy, it's your personal responsibility to ask questions, to get the information you need to get and stay on track. This is a prime responsibility of a Radio-Active Leader.

You may think you're being a pest or squeaky wheel by challenging accepted wisdom - it's better to be a squeaky wheel than to have the train come off the tracks. Demand honest input from the group around you and offer frank and concise comments whenever possible. Then, and this is critical, once a decision is made, by you, a peer, or a supervisor, support that decision to the best of your ability. Period! Radioactive leaders are decision supporters, process enablers, and champions of group causes. RadioActive Leaders are not whiners, complainers, and general malcontents.

Radioactive Leadership Value #3
Respect

While frankness and candor are important, the method by which they are implemented is equally vital. Respect for each member of the team is not just a good idea, it also increases productivity - people produce more and higher quality results when they feel valued and appreciated. In the short term, the whip may get speed out of the mule, after enough time, it will also kill him.

Rules of respect must be outlined and operational within your sphere of influence:

Whatever the disagreement - the team is more important than the problem.

Personal opinions are acceptable - personal attacks are never permissible.

Treat everyone on your team better than you want to be treated.
Analyze rather than criticize.

Take note of this last point. When leading teams, it's useful to establish criteria for success - your mission objectives - then review results based on the fulfillment of the criteria. Personal opinions are always useful, but not the best barometer for success. Keep team members' judgments within these guidelines:

Does it work?
Does it achieve our objectives?

As opposed to:

I like it.
I don't like it.

Personal opinions are important but, by definition, are subject to interpretation and argument. Objective criteria may be a better gauge of mission fulfillment - and contain less inflammatory reasoning.

Radioactive Leadership Value #4
Be of Service

Great leaders serve great causes. Great leaders assist their teams. The function of a leader is to show the way, to clear the path for others to follow. Leaders are passionately committed to the success of their teams - leaders do not have a function if their teams do not succeed.

Growth can only come through giving - by supplying those around you with the direction and means to achieve their goals. This is where we may find a fundamental misunderstanding in the application of leadership:

Good leaders understand their function is to serve the group. Bad leaders assume the group must serve them.

This cart-before-the-horse problem can kill a team before it even gets started. There is no alternative - leaders must serve the group.

Radioactive Leadership Value #5
A Lifetime of Self-Improvement

Leaders never stop learning or exploring; leaders always look to add to their knowledge and expertise. In the profession of leadership, comprehensive knowledge is useful, if not vital. You may not have to know everything, but you will need to know what you're missing.

A fundamental precept of successful teamwork is requesting (or demanding) individual members bring their unique knowledge for the group's applications and study. The next precept requires members continue to acquire knowledge and expertise to provide more useful materials to the group. Michael Jordan, already the greatest basketball player of his era, spent countless hours in mid-career developing his jump shot and 3 point shot. The more weapons he could bring to each game, the better he and his team would be.

Radioactive Leadership Value #6
Emotional Self-Reliance

If you're expecting a pat on the back for a job well done - unless you can pat your own back, you're going to be waiting a long time. In the cutthroat pace of today's economic reality, rewards for superior performance are fewer and farther between. A raise or promotion is always possible but please don't count on it - there's an equal likelihood of getting laid off next week. This isn't necessarily a reflection on you - it's just the nature of today's business beast.

The flip side of the coin is - there are organizations that have good reward and recognition programs, but simply don't use them. For many reasons, the people in position to trigger these rewards don't award them.

In the face of this conflict: success without reward, RA Leaders *must learn to provide their own rewards!* No kidding. You've got to be able to reward yourself, meaningfully, for a job well done. Your own opinion of yourself must mean as much, or more, to you as any external opinion.

In order to lead, as much as you've got to know when to kick yourself in the behind, you also have to know when to pat yourself on the back - and you must do both with equal amounts of critical accuracy.

Business reality of the day: they'll line up around the block to kick your behind... and then disappear when you deserve the medal.

"So what?" you say. So - shape your expectations to fit your needs. Change your behavior so you don't require approval or applause from others to do superior work. Care about your own opinion as much or more than any other - depend on yourself for your own congratulations and commiserations. Through this self-reliance you begin to free yourself from the cravings of external approval.

Radioactive Leadership Value #7
Provide Encouragement and Support

As Leader there will come a time when you are the only source of support for your entire group. Especially during times of high activity and stress, teams need support like the crops need water. The more demanding the situation, the more support is required. This support extends to every sort of business interaction: time, materials, attention, concentration, money and more. As important as those items are, emotional support is just as crucial.

It's important to provide encouragement on an individual as well as team basis. A private word of praise can mean as much to a stressed-out team member as anything you can provide. On the other hand, a consistent lack of encouragement tears at the identity and heart of any team.

The rule is: cynicism comes from a lack of encouragement - sincere support is the anti-cynicism. Even the most pessimistic team members need some sort of affirmation - and, as always, it's up to YOU to provide it.

Radio - Activities

"Let no man imagine that he has no influence. Whoever he may be, and wherever he may be placed, the man who thinks becomes a light and a power."

- Henry George

RadioActive Leaders know, by instinct or otherwise, that leadership has its responsibilities, its demands, and its rewards. Great leaders understand that the moment of "taking charge" is preceded by a lifetime of preparation. Every great leader, Gandhi or Gates, Moses or Mozart - each of them spent a lifetime in preparation of their calling, of their passion, of their destiny. They knew what they needed to know and were ready to use that knowledge for themselves and for those around them.

In addition to self awareness and courage, preparation is crucial to RadioActive leadership.

The Goal of Goal-Setting

The first function of goal-setting is to provide yourself a target, an objective or prize you need to acquire. The second function of goal-setting is to provide yourself with criteria - so that you know, with full certainty, you've accomplished what you wanted to achieve. These purposes are more important than they first appear, more important than you might imagine. You'd be stunned to know how much effort is wasted by people working hard without knowing why they're working hard. This might seem to contradict common sense; but trust me, in business and many other places - common sense is not all that common.

Many people, with superior skills, fail in the execution of their missions for lack of proper goal setting. They simply don't know how to, or can't, set goals that are:

a) Attainable
b) On target
c) Worthwhile

Why? Because many people with superior skills fail to realize that goals that are attainable, on target, and worthwhile are simply problems out of focus. Think about that for a moment. A salesperson complains to a peer that the communications about the current sale were not timely, the items on sale do not have the right price points on them, and "everything is screwed up, how do 'THEY' expect us to make any money?" The truth of the matter is this particular sales person reads his email two days late consistently, fails to sign the sales items properly and is, in general, a poor sales performer. Sound familiar? So let us put this problem in focus:

· Put up the right signing - NOW

· Read your emails - NOW

· Stop blaming others - NOW

See, the problems in focus become your goals. Inside of each and every problem you will ever face, personally and professionally, lies the goals that you want to seek as a Radioactive

Leader. Think of problems as diamonds in the rough (Theme music from Disney's *Aladdin* is playing in my head right now). Truly understanding the problem's effect on team productivity or mission accomplishment allows us to truly begin the goal setting process. Use the following RadioActive Leadership Resolution Plan to work through a specific problem you and/or your team is facing. At each step, the goal should become clearer.

Radioactive Leadership Resolution Plan

Use this outline to map the problems and resolutions your team will face.

 Identify the Issue

What is the central problem? (Define the subject, when and how it occurs.)

_____

_____

_____

_____

Who does it affect? (Be specific with people impacted by the problem: delivery, stock, sales, management, etc.)

_____

_____

_____

_____

_____

_____

How does it affect them? (Be clear about concerns that arise from the problem: can't find orders, difficulty organizing, late with inventory, etc.)

_____

_____

_____

_____

_____

_____

What are the specific consequences of the problem? (Problems in communication, customers not getting correct order, bad for morale, etc.)

_____

_____

_____

_____

Brainstorm possible solutions. (Review all options. Brainstorm far and wide. No judgments on solutions until you've finished this part of the creative process. Keep it simple.)

_____

_____

_____

_____

_____

_____

Action items. (Define roles and responsibilities - who can help and in what areas. Assign actions and dates for future reference. Make sure everyone knows their responsibilities and deliverables. Make sure you accept as much responsibility as anyone else. Help team members as needed. Watch as individual team members apply their unique talents. Give lots of praise along the way.)

Action/ Person *(What to do and who's doing it)*	**Short Term** *(Date and deliverable - once the action is taken what will the result look like)*	**Medium Term** *(Date and deliverable - once the action is taken what will the result look like)*	**Long Term** *(Date and deliverable - once the action is taken what will the result look like)*

Results and assessment. (How did the group work? Was the problem solved? Were results achieved? What is the benefit of the activity?)

Problem	Resolution	Results

The Responsibility of Personal Progress - Knowing

"What we actually learn, from any given set of circumstances, determines whether we become increasingly powerless or more powerful."

- Blaine Lee

How much can you learn? How much can you know?

The answer to the second question is easier than the first. You can know everything you need to know. It's out there. All the answers to every question in the universe - each answer, every solution exists somewhere in space and time. Some problems may take more time than others - curing the common cold or creating a light beer that doesn't taste like foamy rust, for example. But, as sure as every problem has its answer, they are out there.

The universe is full of magical things, patiently waiting for our wits to grow sharper."

- Eden Phillpotts

Given that every riddle can be solved, the ability to find the solution lies in your investment of time, energy and commitment. If you are willing, you are able. If you choose to do it, it will be done. The opposite is also true.

❊ *Ability = Commitment* ❊

It's a simple formula - if you want to do something, and do it well, you must commit to it without regard to obstacles, challenges or setbacks. You can sail a boat or repair an artery; you can run a marathon or run for office. The only limitation is in your desire and commitment.

In order to increase your leadership effectiveness, you need to know everything you can know about your field - without regard to perceived limitations. Knowledge and authority go hand in hand - if you accept responsibility, or even have it thrust on you, your comprehensive knowledge is one key to assure success. Competence and understanding build respect - great leaders understand this relationship. As you

60

aspire to RadioActive Leadership, the continuous enhancement of your knowledge base will also expand your ability to lead.

Now to the first question - how much can you learn? The answer to this question is a little trickier. As we've seen, all the information you need is out there, waiting for someone to go get it. Learning, on the other hand, is not just an activity but also a way of life. The ability to learn is quite different from the desire to learn. And in the case of learning, there is no substitute for desire. Study skills, high IQ, memory retention, access to classes - none of these qualities can take the place of true desire to learn.

Take this moment, right now, to create an analysis of the skills and information, the talents and abilities you need to become a Radioactive Leader.

RadioActive Leadership
Aptitude Assessment

Why are you here?
At this job:

In this world:

What do you want?
From life in general:

From your career overall:

From this job in particular:

What do you need?
How much money:

What kind of responsibilities:

What sort of opportunities:

How far do you want to go:

Here's a list of questions to assess more areas of development - as well as thought-starters for areas of improvement to achieve full RA Leadership:

1. Would I like to work with someone like me?

2. Would I like to have a boss like me?

3. Would I like others to support me like I support them?

4. Do people know who I am?

5. Am I someone others seek for advice and ideas?

6. Is my expertise known to others?

7. Do I continuously enhance my skills? Do I build on my strengths?

8. Do I have a personal vision for my life and work?

9. Is my vision in sync with my values?

10. Have I communicated my vision to others?

11. Do I have high standards for myself and others?

12. Am I the benchmark for getting results at my job?

13. Do others ask me how I do what I do?

14. Do I expect as much from myself as I do others?

15. Do I work toward new results every day?

16. Am I passionate about something? Do I know what I want?

17. Do I get excited? Embrace each day? Do I hit the ground running?

18. Do I seek out positive people?

19. Do I see life as a kid? An attitude of expectation? Something new?

20. Is my attitude contagious?

21. By this time next year, I'll be known for ___?

22. I want to be famous for _____?

23. My personal power lies in _____?

24. My most important personal trait is _____?

25. Write down 20 words that describe you:

1	2	3
4	5	6
7	8	9
10	11	12
13	14	15
16	17	18
19	20	

The Purpose of Purpose

"A great deal of talent is lost to the world for want of a little courage. Every day sends to their graves obscure men whose timidity prevented them from making an effort."

- Sidney Smith

You don't have it easy - you work in what used to be politely called the "blue-collar" sector, working your behind off just to keep ahead of the bills. Now you've been labeled an "associate" or "team member" or some other odd designation. It's likely that your prospects for advancement are narrow and intensely competitive - in the current position you hold. You can go back to school or get specialized training - these options will certainly help you get ahead. But mostly, you will have to rely on your own guts and brains to move up. This is the world of business today and tomorrow and it's not a bad condition - you've got possibilities or you're going to make them for yourself.

Here's the thing:

In the odd world in which we live, many organizations are constructed to prevent or impede the possibility of significant advancement - you're just not going to see a lot of millionaire postal workers or extravagantly prosperous kindergarten teachers. It's not built into the process; the rewards for talented professionals in these careers must come from other sources. Having made that point, this isn't to say that there's NO possibility for progress: postal workers become post office managers and teachers become principals, up the ladder we go.

Our main point is that many institutions create conditions that resist the prospects for advancement. These conditions must not be allowed to stifle your desire or ability to move ahead, to fulfill every ounce of potential you possess. You simply can't allow the place to inhibit the person - I won't let you.

You must create, understand and imbed

your own mission at your job and in your life. You must design and implement your own purpose in business and in life.

So, ask yourself, right here and now, "What is my purpose?" I would like to hear it - send me an email at royalston@radioactiveleadership.com.

Assessment

As you may have guessed by now, RadioActive Leadership depends heavily on self-awareness: a keen understanding of your strengths, weaknesses, talents and gaps. Ironically, sometimes it helps to look at yourself from the outside to see what's on the inside. You might be the best judge of your own abilities - and then again, you might not be the best judge. But no matter how good you are at self-assessment, you must become better at it!

RA Leaders know their strengths and weaknesses - they know what to emphasize and what needs attention. They're aware of talents and sensitive to drawbacks - with equal understanding. RA Leaders have the ability to be objective about their abilities - judging them with dispassionate reasoning with the certainty that they're far from perfect. They know there's always room for improvement and they look to the people around them to help with that development. They're not embarrassed or shy about their needs - they know what they need and they go get it.

RA Leaders go back to school or get additional training - both excellent areas of reassessment. RA Leaders know they don't know everything - they don't try to know everything. But they do try to know everything they can, everything they need to know plus a bit more.

Looking at yourself, objectively and realistically, can be more difficult than it sounds. But it's a necessary step in the path to radioactive leadership.

Earlier in the book, we asked you to do some soul searching on what you needed to improve on. Now, I am going to provide to you a list of qualities displayed by radioactive leaders. What I want you to do is determine if the characteristic listed is strength or developmental need for you. Return to the Awareness/Identification model in Chapter 2 and work through updating the online personal progress contract that you created.

Rate yourself - strength or weakness - in the following areas:

	Strength	Weakness
❀ Motivation		
❀ Enthusiasm		
❀ Intelligence		
❀ Practical skills		
❀ Flexible attitude		
❀ Assertiveness		
❀ Communication abilities		
❀ Integrity		
❀ Sincerity		
❀ Sense of humor		
❀ Persistence		

	Strength	Weakness
Patience		
Tolerance		
Cooperation		
Organizational abilities		
Vision		

Knowledge First, Training Second

"Develop a passion for learning. If you do, you'll never cease to grow."
— *D'Angelo*

For our purposes, we define knowledge as the information needed to achieve goals in the short and long term. We define training as the practical application of that knowledge. As we acquire knowledge, it's functional and rehearsed application is as important as the knowledge itself. A great classical pianist who never leaves the practice hall is a talent wasted. Knowledge must lead to application - otherwise the knowledge dies.

Superior training leads to superior results. The opposite is also true. In many forms of crisis training: military, police and fire, medical, etc., it is a well known concept that poor training produces lack of confidence which leads to misunderstanding and misdirection at best;

at its worst, poor training produces panic and disaster. A RadioActive Leader takes responsibility for his training, at every level, regardless of the obstacles or challenges - and regardless of the resources provided or absent. A Radio-Active Leader recognizes training as an investment in personal assets, and the precise means to control his own destiny. In much the same way smart people invest in mutual funds or savings accounts, IRAs and real estate, a RadioActive Leader invests in his own education and training.

Authority and Responsibility

Okay, this subject is a tricky one. Here's the first rule:

You must never accept responsibility without the authority to execute it.

"What?" I hear you say. So I'll say it again - never accept responsibility without the authority to execute it. This may seem to run contrary to the basic principles of RadioActive

Leadership; it does not. RadioActive Leaders understand the scope of their responsibilities very clearly. They may choose to expand that scope and include more tasks and goals, but good leaders are realistic about their ability to execute the undertaking they accept.

Great leaders take time to accurately analyze the mission before them. They estimate and understand the resources needed to accomplish the mission; they know they must delegate important tasks and established checkpoints to ensure tasks are accomplished. Great leaders understand that communication and execution go hand in hand.

Being realistic about the responsibility you accept is as important as the fulfillment of the overall mission. For example, a district manager asks you to lead a team of associates to brainstorm the design of a new point of sale display. You're smart and talented; you've shown initiative and have produced great results in other projects. You're perfect for this sort of assignment.

Unfortunately, the manager has included several people on your team from other stores and you have no authority over their schedule or participation. Now you're faced with the dilemma: an important task to achieve without the tools to accomplish it. For some of you, this may seem a strange circumstance - a manager expecting results without providing the tools to get those results. For other readers, this situation is part of your everyday work life.

Examples of
RadioActive Leadership

"Setting an example is not the main means of influencing others; it is the only means."

- Albert Einstein

In this chapter, we're going to share with you stories of RadioActive Leaders who changed the world around them. These people are not famous or rich (yet) - they are simply the ones who chose to do more than expected, to work to improve their surroundings and their teams. Most important - these people are exactly like you. They didn't have any special training or privileges; no one gave them a head-start - they didn't wait for permission: they went out and worked with what they had to make their lives better. In short, they are RadioActive Leaders.

Jan Greene
Child Protective Service,
Indianapolis, Indiana

Jan Greene is a social worker, dealing with some of the most difficult circumstances in our society: poverty, racism, poor opportunities for the residents of her area. Like many people in her calling, Jan works to make society better and she usually works toward that goal one person at a time. Jan is also challenged by many conditions typical in large bureaucracies: understaffed, overworked, endless paperwork, lack of recognition or advancement, etc. (Sounds a little like your job, doesn't it?) The sheer volume of work is enough to frustrate a saint.

At the time of our story, Jan had been working at CPS for just under five years. It was her first job out of community college and she was committed to helping children in crisis. CPS seemed to be the perfect place to carry out her mission. Child Protective Service is a very large bureaucracy - and it runs like you might expect: glacially slow, mountains of red tape and an incomprehensible maze of organizational layers. At the time, when CPS was in the news, it was rarely good. Case after case of poor follow-up resulting in children left in unsafe environments - a string of stories too numerous and unfortunate to list. Newspapers were having a field day lambasting the agency for its poor performance.

Dedicated and caring, Jan was becoming increasingly frustrated with the bureaucratic grinding that prevented her from doing what she thought was right - and she was equally tired of the continual stream of negative press.

It was a typical work day; Jan was lunching with some of her co-workers when one spoke up, "I don't care what the media says - they always have negative things to say about us anyway. I have been with CPS for 22 years and it's never going to change - too may cases and not enough case workers. We can't possibly save every child from crazy or lazy parents and the lousy environments the kids grow up in."

The group nodded heads in silent agreement as the woman went on, "No one appreciates what we do - half the city doesn't even know we exist and the other half resents us. When you try to change things, you get knocked right back down because of some b.s. rules. I gave up trying long ago...just let me make it to retirement!" As the other case workers added their agreement, Jan felt frustrated, almost ill.

Jan faced the grim facts. As she was traveling home, she asked herself, "Why am I at CPS? What brought me here in the first place? Can I seriously have a positive impact on my 85 current cases?" Jan began to think of all the reasons why she could not succeed - and tried to reconcile that she was simply not going to succeed - so why even worry about it. In her mind, she conceded, "It is what it is. It was the same before I got here; it will be the same when I'm gone."

So Jan coasted. She put in her time and did her work, but she didn't do anything more than she had to do. She was going to get along with her work, but that was it.

One day she opened the newspaper to discover a story of an 11 year old boy beaten to death by his mother's boyfriend. Apparently, the boyfriend slammed young Marcus' head into a wall, killing him. The mother and boyfriend tried to cover it up - offering that the death was accidental.

Compounding the atrocity of Marcus' death was the fact that his CPS case worker hadn't been to the home in 4 years. During that time, there had been 27 documented complaints of child abuse and neglect. Marcus had been let down by his family, his neighbors and CPS as well. As fate would have it, his case worker was the very same one who'd complained in the lunch room at CPS.

Jan went home that night and was angry, mad that such a thing could happen, mad that CPS had failed. Then Jan started to think about her own cases - she had been coasting and she knew it. This could very well have been one of the children in her cases. Jan's anger turned to fear; not for herself, but for her cases and children. She knew that she was coasting because everyone else at CPS was doing the same. The prevailing attitude at CPS was one of fully negative expectations - no one really expects us to make a huge difference, the system is set against us, so just take care of the minimum requirements.

Then Jan had her epiphany - she realized that she was allowing her work environment to fully affect her attitude and control her performance. Emotions of anger and fear, frustration and apathy became operating strategies and Jan, to her dismay, realized she'd let herself be dragged into these methods. She also realized that this mind set must change immediately - or another human being, a child, a family, would be the ones to suffer. Jan knew she had the power to change this situation and she took it upon herself to start at that moment.

She called her best friend and told her all that had been happening at CPS, the story of Marcus and what she was feeling. Her friend agreed that Jan had a choice to make - either do the job to the best of her ability or not do the job at all. Jan's friend added, "Whatever you decide to do is your choice, but be ready for the consequences. Also, give a lot of thought to the environment you work in. I mean, why are you allowing it to control you as opposed to you controlling it? You're smarter than that and you care more than that. OK!" Jan decided to make a change to her life that very moment. The next day, she went to her office early and began to re-evaluate each and every one of her cases. Though she hadn't been to a home is some time, Jan made a schedule of visits to review each case in person.

Over the next few weeks, Jan ate lunch at her desk in order to prioritize her case load based visit schedules, documented complaints and severity of conditions. She determined that 27 cases were critical priority - in need of immediate attention. Jan explained to her supervisor her new aggressive plan for home visits. When Jan requested she start from home to maximize her case time, her supervisor disagreed. "No. Too may people have abused that process in the past. Start from here so I know you are working." Jan was stung by the supervisor's response, but she shook it off and remained determined to follow her overall plan.

Jan came to work early and left work late. Over the course of the next week, she was able to conduct 16 in-depth home visits. The workload was daunting; the obstacles were immense. But Jan kept saying to herself, "One child at a time. One child at a time." She reassured herself that the schedule was not as important as the effect she was having on each person she worked with.

A few days later, a co-worker stopped Jan on her way out and asked where Jan had been. "We've been missing you at lunch." Jan explained her plan to do 27 home visits in a week. She'd only finished 16 but would finish the rest into next week. The co-worker frowned and said, "You're making the rest of us look bad. Are you sucking up or something?" The co-worker walked away, leaving Jan to her hurt and rejection. Even through the frustration, Jan resolved not to be swayed by the disapproval. She got in her car, reached for her map route of homes and said out loud, "Where is my first client?"

It took Jan two weeks to finish her priority visits - but the crisis strategy paid off. Jan removed two little boys from a filthy crack house. The boys had been subjected to abuse and suffered from malnutrition. The two boys received much needed medical attention and were placed in emergency foster care.

Through her new schedule, Jan's co-workers grumbled and talked about her. Rumors flew about Jan's motives and reasoning. In spite of the pessimism, frustration and jealousy, Jan felt proud of her accomplishment and grateful for her new optimism and energy. She remembered her own rule, "One child at a time."

Jan did not receive any formal acknowledgment for her work - her supervisor did make one comment about Jan's overtime. As she progressed though, Jan discovered that her prioritizing of cases actually made her more efficient - she was getting a lot of work done. As important, Jan was starting to feel good about her work.

Suspicious at first, her coworkers started to ask about her workload - some even thought the supervisor was giving her less to do. Jan shared her daily planner and method of prioritizing that allowed her to personally "touch" all of her cases. Co-workers began to implement some of the ideas and Jan found herself leading sessions with co-workers, showing them how she planned her workload. It was immensely rewarding, seeing others following her plans. Mike, a recent hire who had talked to Jan about quitting, warmed to the process right away. He began following Jan's system and was starting to feel better about his performance and job.

Other co-workers began to seek Jan out and ask her advice on cases and individual clients. She found herself in brainstorming lunches with different groups of associates.

These chat sessions focused on how people overcame bureaucratic obstacles to get things done more effectively and efficiently - which was better for each family and child. The results paid off in short and long term benefits.

During a team meeting, the supervisor related how the number of home visits had drastically increased and the amount of complaints from clients and the public had drastically decreased. While the supervisor offered, "Keep up the good work!" Jan thought about the pictures on the wall in her cubicle of the children she had taken from awful homes and moved them to caring foster families. The supervisor moved on to complaining about expenses, but to her own shock, Jan's great outlook would not go away.

Jan Greene became a force of profound good. She positively impacts the lives of countless children and helped the careers of many talented CPS employees. Her reputation growing through her superior efforts and results, Jan was offered the directorship of a private nonprofit agency dedicated to helping children in need. Reverting for a moment to her old way of thinking, Jan was convinced that she was too young for the job; she was certain she needed more experience. The current director, soon to retire, assured her she was perfect for the position - she was talented and dedicated enough to learn everything she'd ever need to know. The director assured her he'd give her all the help and direction she ever required - it was her dedication that would make the difference.

That agency is now one of the largest and most successful non-profits in Texas. All due to one woman who decided to change herself and the world around her - one child at a time.

❋ What does the story teach?

❋ What do you feel about the story?

✵ What happened and why?

✵ What did Jan do?

✵ What was the result?

✵ What specific RA Leadership traits did Jan embrace?

✵ What was her lasting impression on the team?

✵ What happened to Jan?

Fernando Garcia
From Target Team Member
To Target Executive Team Leader

Earlier in my career, I ran two stores for Target, the wonderful retail chain. Both stores were staffed with potentially great team members - any one of which had the ability and desire to lead and lead well. I created a challenge for the executive team: create a plan to develop floor team members into executive team leaders. The basic concept was twofold: incent and inspire executive teams to train lower-level workers into upper-level positions and to identify and nurture retail associates who exhibit superior management skills.

Target was continuing an aggressive growth strategy and sought to cultivate talent from within its own ranks - an excellent policy that benefits both the bottom line and corporate culture.

It was during this program that I met one of the greatest team members I've ever encountered. I'd like to tell you his story. Fernanado

Garcia is a young man from Miami. He worked on the back room team - his everyday mission was to do the best possible job, help the store succeed and grow with its success. Fernando did not have the greatest command of the English language but he had heart, determination and the will to lead and succeed.

Our executive team began interviewing team members at every level for training and accelerated development for executive leadership positions in our district. Fernando was one of the first associates to take the challenge. Actually, he jumped at the challenge.

Fernando brought considerable abilities to the table: his per-hour productivity was one of the best in the store, he was adept at every process and procedure and best of all, Fernando was the sort of associate everyone went to for answers and ideas - the model of a "get it done" kind of person. The only thing Fernando lacked was a path to follow; it was up to us to build that path for him.

Our accelerated development program

focused on teaching team members practical lessons of entry-level supervision: interviewing skills, coaching techniques, consensus building and decision making, among many other important competencies. As we worked with each selected individual, our goal was to see who would distinguish themselves from the others - who would show not just the fundamental abilities to lead, but also the talent and desire as well.

As the stores' team leader, I paid close attention to the people in the accelerated development program. As RadioActive Leaders do, it was my goal to train my own replacement as I moved up in the chain of command. My midterm plan was to train people who would surpass my own pretty solid levels of productivity and efficiency.

It was both exciting and rewarding to watch Fernando as he developed into a truly RadioActive Leader. While it began subtly, immediate signs of progress were noticed: increased shift productivity, a marked rise in volunteers for tough sets and store transitions and dramatic increases in store team meetings. Associates saw Fernando as one of them - wanting to do well for him - and also a model of their own future successes. He made himself available to everyone, pitching in wherever needed, and his teams responded by pitching in with him in every shift.

One day, as I was walking through the back room, I noticed a team huddle - Fernando was in the center of the group, demonstrating the proper use of a new LRT (handheld scanner). The group worked through all the intricacies of the process, with demonstration and trials, in mere minutes - a session that would have taken us hours in the past. Fernando trained the group with confidence and full authority. Later, several associates explained Fernando had started "teaching moments" where processes and procedures were shown and practiced - experienced associates showing newer members the ropes and techniques. So many new members had come to him with questions;

he decided to open the training for everyone on the shift. He also confessed he learned a lot from associates who'd developed their own efficiencies.

Fernando started this program on his own - meeting needs with uncommon sense and excellent leadership. Fernando's manager pointed out he'd started it to solve problems, share knowledge and, he did it all on his own - he started his own cycle of RadioActivity, enhancing not just the performance and efficiency of each associate, but also increasing the production of the entire store.

Through the "teaching moments" he'd instituted, Fernando himself was soon able to master every key function of the back room and inventory processes. Fernando and the people on his shift were sought out by other stores to teach procedures and teaching moment techniques. With the success of the processes and store productivity, we recommended Fernando begin training at executive level leadership.

Given a leadership position in a new

store, Fernando expanded his ideas and excelled within the new challenges and responsibilities. While I very much wanted to keep Fernando in my store, I recognized his potential for greater opportunities - and I returned to my goal of training people who could take my place, making me that much more valuable in my own progress. With these thoughts in mind, Fernando was on his way.

In the course of my two years at these stores, we trained seven team members to become executives in other stores - our reputation was the store that grew executives. In fact, we built RadioActive Leaders: people who thrived through opportunity, who flourished even as they provided advancement for everyone around them. We trained these RA Leaders to understand that they could influence others by leading themselves first. We built RA Leaders who won over their peers through perseverance, street smarts and optimism.

I am proud to have been a part of it.

✺ What does the story teach?

✺ What do you feel about the story?

✺ What happened and why?

✺ What did Fernando do?

✺ What was the result?

✳ What specific RA Leadership traits did Fernando embrace?

✳ What was his lasting impression on the team?

✳ What happened to Fernando?

Golden Rules
of RA Leadership

"No pressure? No diamonds."
- Mary Case

The problem with common sense in business is that it is never common and doesn't always make sense. There are many principles, concepts that should be general practice in business, which are either casually ignored or categorically rejected in the everyday course of our work lives. RA Leaders combat ignorance or lazy thinking by implementing common sense strategies of their own. They study and embrace rules which assist them in success.

Here are some principles offered as planning elements for your list.

The Golden Rules

 Respect every person you contact
Provide respect before you have any

expectations. RA Leaders assume they must demonstrate respect and deference to the people around them.

RA Leaders don't wait to see if respect is required or demanded, they offer it as their operating routine.

Include everyone

If they are within your reach and sphere of influence, they must be included in all workings of the group. Nothing kills morale quicker than the suspicion (or reality) that a person is being excluded from a team function. Exclusion is a double-edged sword - both individual and team morale suffers.

Treat everyone BETTER than you want to be treated

In business, the expectations of personal treatment may be low even before we begin. Sometimes we, ourselves, set the bar so low that we're grateful for any level of civility or positive behavior. RA Leaders don't respond to behavior - they establish behavior for themselves and the people around them. RA Leaders radiate excellence in personal dealings.

 ### *If you have something good to say...*

It is ***your responsibility to say it!*** Never hold back a compliment or encouragement - never stifle an idea or the suggestion of a better way to achieve a goal. Shyness or insecurity is no excuse - RA Leaders must lead.

 ### *If you have something bad to say...*

It is ***your responsibility to say it - in the context of an open meeting!*** RA Leaders must never, ever complain outside the context of open meetings. They must never say something in private that they wouldn't say in public.

RA Leaders take responsibility for both their words and their actions.

They do not say one thing and do

another.

 ## *Withstand the slings and arrows...*

Insecure people gossip and whine - this is a propensity as old as mankind. RA Leaders understand and accept this tendency - and they refuse to allow it to change their self-image or direction. RA Leaders are filled with deep purpose and good intentions - they live what they say and do.

Put credit where credit is due...

RA Leaders are realistic and sensible. They know when a job is done well and RA Leaders aren't shy about offering or sharing praise with the team around them. RA Leaders immerse their own egos to the needs and aspirations of their team - secure in the knowledge that the success of the team assures their personal success as well.

Expect and accept excellence

Excellence is a way of life - the continual pursuit of a better way, a more valuable contribution.

Serve others

RA Leaders begin with the belief that their purpose is to serve the people around them. Through this service, they will obtain greater benefits and rewards.

Be transparent

The only traits that must be hidden are the ones you want no one to see. RA Leaders are transparent because they have nothing to hide. Become more transparent, more open, more accessible and more genuine. You will grow in proportion to your visibility.

Take responsibility for ALL relationships

Blaming things outside your control

means that you're surrendering responsibility and ability to direct yourself. YOU rule your own actions, directions and results - no one is responsible for you except you. This also means that you can make any relationship work - or allow it to fail. The power is within you - no one else.

As Always, It's Up To You

You may work in a business which rejects the Golden Rules - a place where fear, anger, frustration or resignation governs behavior and productivity. You may work in an environment that stifles creativity and risk-taking, a place that suppresses open communication for back-stabbing and power-grabbing. Certainly, there are plenty of places that have these conditions as a normal course of business.

Guess what? The conditions surrounding you don't matter - the environment you're immersed in can't be allowed to change your direction, to alter your purpose or to sway your conviction to lead and succeed. Simply put, you can't let something outside change what's inside - you are the master and creator of your mood, your attitude and your future. RA Leaders radiate attitudes that assist them in achieving their goals - they bring their own position to the table. They refuse to let someone or something derail them or negatively influence their purpose or direction.

The Golden Rules aren't offered as some sort of abstract advice - these are laws that help you become more effective, expand your abilities and influence and make you more successful. If you live them, you will see - if you reject them, you won't.

Next Step - Do This NOW

Start now - choose two RadioActive Leadership Golden Rules and start applying them in your life right now. Repeat until each Rule becomes a natural part of your operating system, your routine, your life. And email me at royalston@radioactiveleadership.com - tell me how it's going. I can also help with about a million tips to implement these Rules and many more.

The BE Story

To this point in our book, we've told you a lot of things: what to do, how to do it, what to try, things to work on, etc. The directions we've provided are important, necessary and fundamental to your comprehension and growth as a RadioActive Leader. In matter-of-fact terms (as clear as we can make them), we've shown proven traits and behaviors that build capability as a leader and success in business. We've examined success stories and reviewed success strategies. In short, we've told you what to do and how to do it.

Now you must decide what you are going to be. You should now begin to write your own "Who Am I Going To Be" story. Here are some questions to help you construct the story that will become your personal future:

Will you be the person who has respect for every person you come into contact with? Will you automatically provide appreciation for the people around you - those you know well and those you don't know at all? Can you lose your skepticism and gain more sincerity? Will you choose to be this person?

Will you be the person who includes everyone in your process? Will you be the one that makes sure everyone is involved, active and listened to? Will you show respect to people whose opinion differs from yours? Can you give the benefit of the doubt - and can you benefit by learning from other people?

Will you be secure enough to admit you don't know everything? Will you be the one to ask for help?

Will you be the first person to offer help to someone who doesn't know as much as you do? Will you welcome the new people and invite the strangers into your group?

Will you be the person who treats people

better than you are treated? Will you set the standard for excellent behavior and incredible character?

Will you be the first person to compliment a job well done? Will you be the one who always gives the pat on the back and tells the boss how other people did a great job? Will you be the first to put credit where it's due? Will you rally other people to a job well done?

Will you be the person who helps out when a job is not getting done? Will you be the one to lend a hand, while also sharing your concerns?

Will you have the courage to point out the problems that already exist? Will you be the one to brainstorm ideas and offer solutions - even risking solutions that may not work? Do you have the judgment and discretion to point out problems and flaws - without harming another person? Will you point out the concerns that no one else will show? Can you be straightforward enough, courageous enough to show your concern while also fixing the problem?

Will you be the one who has the courage to withstand negativity - the slings and arrows of pessimistic people? Can you stand up to bullies or whiners? Will you turn unconstructive situations into productive results?

Will you be the one who strives for excellence? Are you the one who will insist on it in your work? Will you encourage excellence in everyone around you?

Will you serve others while you take care of yourself? Will you be of service whenever and wherever possible?

Will you gladly learn as much as you can? Will you become a full-time student of your craft? Will you encourage learning in everything you do and with everyone in your group?

Will you be the person who arrives first and leaves last? Will you be the one to start the project, gather the team? Will you be the one that gets things started and the one who gets things done?

Will you be the person who gets along

with everyone? Can you be the one who everyone goes to? Will you lead by example and
make sure your example is superior? Can you
take responsibility for all your personal and professional relationships?

Are you the person that can change your
world, a little bit at a time, to make it what it's
supposed to be? Can you make your corner of
the world a little better, a little smarter? Can
you leave your world a lot better off than you
found it?

Can you handle what you have to do? Are
you sensible enough to separate the important
stuff from the other stuff? Can you prioritize
your work and your life?

Can you make your family more important than your work? Can you make your
work more important than your play? Will you
choose to love the life you choose to live?

Will you coach others to be better than
they are? Will you coach others to be better
than you? Will you lead people for the pure joy
of seeing them succeed? Will you lead yourself

in the same way?

Will you be the peacemaker, the one who helps settle issues and resolve problems? Can you help people see the other side of the problem? Will you help everyone find the solution?

Will you fully develop yourself - to explore your potential to its fullest abilities? Will you continue to add knowledge and understanding? Will your nurture your talents while addressing your shortcomings?

Will you accept responsibility? Will you accept challenges? Will you be the one to volunteer? Will you be the first to raise your hand?

Will you lead?

Let's see how you'll do...

The following concepts are scenarios that challenge your current ideas of accurate direction and are designed to challenge you to apply what you're learned so far.

Retail

If you're like most humans, your very worst customer service experiences happen in a few main places:

1. Phone "help" lines
2. Retail stores
3. City Hall
4. The bank
5. Utility company

Okay, there are LOTS of places where you might receive terrible service: fast food restaurants, virtually any municipal department, airlines, etc. For our purposes, we'll narrow the focus a bit. Please extrapolate these exercises to best fit your own situation.

Take a moment to remember the worst moments you have ever had shopping at your retail or outlet store. There is nothing more dismaying or irritating than unknowledgeable, unmotivated, and uncaring store employees. In a strange turn of shopping experiences: the very purpose of a store employee is to help customers - the reason people have jobs in stores is to help the customers that come into those stores.

Yes, this sounds almost silly in its simplicity - but you would be stunned to discover how many employees don't consider the customer their first responsibility. If you talk to employees in the retail world and ask them to list their job responsibilities, many of them will never even mention the customer! Strange, but very true.

So we agree - retail stores need help in every area of leadership.

Now, imagine you work at a local "big-box" discount store - you are now the employee. It's the busiest time of the day and you're on your way to lunch (bag in hand). You walk past the cash registers - there are only two lanes open and about fifty people waiting to get rung up. You hear a customer grumble, "I can't believe this big a$% store has 30 registers and only two of them are open!"

What do you do?

a) Continue on to lunch
b) Tell the store manager
c) Tell someone else to help out
d) Tell the customer to pipe down and wait
e) Open a new register yourself
f) Turn and go the other way avoiding the register area all together

This is not a trick question, though it may seem to be one. The answer is b) Tell the store manager. Their job is to manage the resources of the store accurately and efficiently - and for whatever reason, those resources are not being allocated correctly.

Some of you assumed the answer was e) Open a new register yourself. You get a star for initiative but a B for brains. Opening a new register might mitigate the immediate problem, but it doesn't solve the greater overall issue: there are not enough registers open and no one seems to recognize the problem except the customers.

Once you've told the manager, you can certainly volunteer to assist on a new register - never a bad idea to help out, be an example for others and maybe even score some points - but it's actually more important to identify the overall problem to someone who can fix it both short and long term. Remember, we are pursuing excellence *and* influencing the behavior of others.

IMPORTANT NOTE: a good manager will not only take immediate action to resolve the problem: call for cashiers to open new registers, they will also go to a new register themselves to assist customers. This simple action is very useful for several reasons - but the most important reason is that the long line of customers will then see manager-level personnel who care enough to resolve the customers' problems. The long-term benefits of this type of action are almost impossible to overstate - customers appreciate demonstrated good service.

At worst, a grumpy customer may not appreciate the good service, but he also won't retain the bad experience forever. There's an old law of retail sales that applies here:

The customer may not remember the good service you provide - but they'll remember a bad experience forever.

You can easily prove this rule yourself: how many bad experiences do you remember? Now how many good experiences do you remember? For most people, the bad experiences outweigh the good ones in volume and detail. Like that old shampoo commercial, if a customer has a bad experience: she'll tell two people and they'll tell two people... and pretty soon you're out of a job.

Retail 2

For our ongoing training and analysis purposes, let's continue with the retail theme.

You're done with lunch and headed back to your work area. You look down the aisle and see a huge spill in the middle of the floor.

What do you do?

- a) Head down another aisle to avoid the spill
- b) Call someone else to clean it up
- c) Ignore it (someone else already has) and keep on walking
- d) Get over there and do something about it
- e) Tell your supervisor

Again, it looks like a trick question and in this case it is. The correct answers are b), d) and e) - at the same time. The issue here is not with inefficient allocation of services or bad customer experiences - this is a safety problem, in addition to the other issues. When it comes to health and safety of customers or co-workers, there can be nothing more important that those elements. The only thing a customer will remember longer than a bad sales experience is an injury in a store. Not only will they remember it, their lawyer will too. And it's probable that someone is going to pay for the problem.

Important Rule: Health and safety first.

This is a good subject for discussion in your areas of influence - safety first. Bring it up with your groups, managers and related personnel. The one problem you may be able to resolve in advance may be the most important one you never face.

Retail 3

Let's suppose you're now at your work station, it's late in the day and you're diligently working through your assigned tasks (we can dream, can't we?). A customer comes to your area, needing assistance for a minor issue. The problem is - you have to get your tasks done or your supervisor is going to be irate.

What do you do?

a) Ignore the customer
b) Tell the customer you are busy and to go to another section
c) Call your supervisor
d) Call someone over to help the customer
e) Help the customer
f) Walk off and wait until the customer leaves

No tricks here. The answer is e) and c) at the same time. The rule is simple: customers just hate being handed off to another associate. Okay, maybe hate is too strong a term, but they sure don't like it. Their logic is: if you can just answer my questions, we can both get on with life. If I have to wait for someone else, my time is wasted.

You've heard the old phrase: the customer is always right? Well, they're not always right, but in this case they sure are. 99% of problems can be handled in mere moments, if you just deal with them immediately. The customer appreciates it and you'll get back to your assignments that much quicker.

Yes, you should let your manager know you've been sidetracked by a customer - they need the information - but they must also understand your first priority is the customer. If they still rip you, buy them a copy of this book and read them the next part:

Hey Manager, Roy says you're an idiot. The customer comes first and if you don't agree, you'll be out on your butt pretty soon anyway - and then the smart person who's reading this to you can take over your job and do it the right way. So there.

That felt pretty good, didn't it? If only real life worked out like that once in a while. Anyway, do the right thing and you'll become known for doing the right thing. If your manager still rips you, still do the right thing.

Retail 4

It's Halloween Night and up until this point, candy sales have been slow. Your store manager has told the whole team that customers are going to wait until the last minute - make sure the candy and promotional areas are full all night. Its 5:30 pm and suddenly customers are a hundred deep in the candy department - and the shelves are being emptied. This isn't your area and, worse yet, the team member assigned to this area is goofing off in the storage room. Your assigned area is not nearly as busy.

What do you do?

- a) Head down another aisle and avoid the Halloween area
- b) Call the person responsible for this area
- c) Tell your supervisor
- d) Pitch in yourself
- e) Tell the store manger
- f) Hide somewhere

Of course we all really want to do f). But you've got three solutions: b), d) and c) and if those don't work, e). There's not much choice here - something's going to melt down if somebody doesn't get to work.

IMPORTANT ISSUE: We encounter one of the tricky areas of RA Leadership - what happens when you have to take control or responsibility? Are you going to be perceived as bossy or pushy or a rat or all of those options?

The short answer is - yes, it's possible. But you still don't have a choice - you have to do the right thing; your motives have to be directed toward solving the most important problem and in this case, it's the lack of attention to customer needs. You have to "own the problem" and take responsibility for its solution. While other people may have difficulty with this - that's their problem, not yours.

You simply have to do the right thing. A wise philosopher once said, "Nothing done for goodness' sake is wasted." In this case,

> by doing the right thing, you've corrected a
> problem. If people have problems with you
> correcting problems, that's their problem.
> Got it?

Municipal 1

Some of the most thankless jobs in the
history of mankind are those in city government
and municipal administration. Simply put, the
problems are plentiful, the jobs are hard and the
compensation is not as rewarding as it might
be.

Occasionally, citizens who have contact
with city employees do not enjoy the best experiences. At virtually every level of governmental
interaction, there is some type of red-tape guar-
anteed to hinder progress - or an entrenched
and ancient employee who simply could not
care if your water bill isn't right.

Now, imagine you are veteran city
employee. You've been working for the water
department for 26 years and there is not one

complaint you haven't heard. To you - it simply doesn't matter that customer satisfaction is low. Heck, it's the water department, you still get paid every other week and you're going to retire in a couple more years.

In a staff meeting, your new supervisor announces there is going to be new focus placed on customer service. "Together, we are going to create a faster, friendlier water department," claims the new supervisor. The new supervisor goes on to lay out an entire customer service plan that involves every worker being available to every customer on the customer's terms. Specifically, there will be no lunch or break during peak times of the day - between 11:00 AM and 2:00 PM.

For the past 13 years, you've been taking your lunch at noon every work day. You're the senior person in the room. And those people who were there before you "earned" their seniority through long years and hard work. You're going to enjoy your seniority just like they did. In response to the news, everyone in the meeting is grumbling. They don't like these new customer service initiatives; some people are even mumbling that they are simply not going to do it.

What do you do?
- a) Continue to take your lunch at noon every work day
- b) Tell your union rep
- c) Join the grumbling employees
- d) Resist each and every change the new supervisor is trying
- e) Work slower and take care of even less customers
- f) Embrace the customer service initiative and set the example

The answer here is simple: f) and b). Yes, you can always talk to your union. But remember, it's your job to be part of the solution, not the other side.

IMPORTANT ISSUE: I'm going to go off on a philosophical tangent here... and I'll begin with an unchallengeable rule of RA Leadership:

YOU MUST NEVER
EQUATE YOUR ACTIONS
WITH COMPENSATION
(or lack thereof)!

To put it more simply: you may NEVER allow your personal circumstances: level of pay, difficulty of job, lack of rewards, etc. - to influence your behavior. You must always do the right thing because it is simply the right thing to do.

Once you begin to rationalize poor behavior on circumstances outside your control - the raise or promotion you didn't get, the recognition you never get, the boss who doesn't like you, etc. - you're sliding down the slippery slope of negative character and destructive results. By permitting yourself to ignore good actions or even by purposefully doing the wrong thing, you've begun the process of failing, giving up and losing. There's no other way to look at it - either you do the right thing or you don't. Being underpaid or underappreciated, though you were passed over for the promotion or switched to a different department - none of those issues are relevant to the current problem!

Imagine the emergency room doctor who provides a sliding scale of service based on how much she made this year - or the firefighter who will only put out half the fire because he got passed over for his promotion. You may think your position doesn't demand the same level of commitment; if you do think that way, you're wrong. The only thing that you take with you is your own self-worth; the only thing you keep is your reputation.

And, when it comes down to doing the right thing, the only solution you can provide is the one in front of you. You can't go back and fix the problem from last year -

but you CAN fix the problem in front of you right now. And positive steps gain us more positive steps - the opposite is also true.

Enough with the rant: back to the scenarios.

Municipal 2

The new water department supervisor is a real go getter. The city has been given a federal grant to convert city government vehicle from gasoline powered vehicles to natural gas vehicles. There isn't a lot of information available and the drivers are not given any say in the matter. (Sound familiar?) There are rumors the converted vehicles are hard to fuel up, drive slower, and have leaks that could make you sick.

The day has come- the vehicles are here. The new supervisor tells the drivers the gas vehicles are gone and the natural gas vehicles are to be used effective immediately. Just a few problems: no one has been trained on the new vehicles. There are no instructions to properly operate them. Without even being told how to fuel them up, the drivers are sent off driving the new vehicles.

Lucky you - you're one of these drivers; *what do you do?*

- a) Refuse to drive the converted vehicle
- b) Openly complain about the new vehicle
- c) Request a transfer from the water department
- d) Request time to self-train on the vehicles
- e) Seek out information on the converted vehicle
- f) Practice operating the vehicles with other drivers

You already know the answers: d), e) and f). Referring back to health and safety - you're going to need at least some time to acclimate yourself to the vehicle.

We'll address a few points with this example. It's obvious to everyone reading this scenario that some really egregious errors have been made by leadership in regards to the roll-out of the new vehicles.

In the workplace, any workplace, are new programs, initiatives, processes, and procedures rolled out with little to no training or communication? YES! It happens all the time; in fact, the times when full training is provided are the rare ones.

RadioActive Leadership does not exist in a vacuum. You must be keenly aware of the communications and execution mechanisms of your organization. (We could write an entire new book on communication and execution in the workplace - but that's the next book.) Being aware of communications and execution will allow you to embrace change without being defeated by the lack of organization within your organization.

As an RA Leader, it's your job to see opportunity, not obstacles!

If Not You - Then Who?

Late at night, when most of us are pretending to be asleep, many people are doing their jobs, delivering newspapers (or babies), cleaning offices, running factory shifts, keeping your town safe, and some people are delivering fresh donuts to go with your morning mocha.

Imagine, for a moment, that you are the overnight donut delivery person. Your job is simple: you've got 17 locations to service. You are to take out the day old donuts and replace them with fresh donuts. You have no other function or responsibility - expected to do nothing else. Your compensation is based on how many donuts are sold per location.

Being the RA Leader you are, you notice that one of your locations does not sell as well as the rest, many donuts are left over. You decide to take a closer look inside the donut case and notice a small hole in the back of the display case. It just may be that flies can get in the case during the day.

What do you do?

> a) Fill the display case with donuts and go to your next location
>
> b) Tell your supervisor
>
> c) Talk to the location owner
>
> d) Stop delivering donuts to the location

Sometimes people who think of themselves as workers or employees do not see the relationship between what they do, day in and day out, and the success or failure of their company.

Some people even contend that they aren't supposed to be concerned with the overall success of their company - that's the job of management, right?

Well, we've arrived at one of the central points of RadioActive Leadership, your responsibility extends to every aspect of your work life. If you can reach it, see it, touch it, smell it, imagine it - then it's YOUR responsibility. (Sometimes it's your responsibility even if you CAN'T do all those things.) The basic principle is: the buck not only stops with you, it also starts and stays moving with you. There's nobody else to push it off on - it's up to you or it doesn't get done. This is the First Commandment of Radio-Active Leadership: *It's Always Up To You, Yourself and No One But You!*

If you don't believe me, just talk to the employees of Montgomery Ward, Venture Department Stores, Enron, Arthur Andersen, TWA or any of the other companies that failed because their parts didn't work or work together. You can accept it or deny it, but the rule is the same: the behavior of every single employee affects the destiny of a company.

So back to the question; what do you do and why?

Write out your answer here then email it to me at royalston@radioactiveleadership.com. I really want to know your answer.

_____

_____

_____

The Department Store

My wife and I were shopping in a large retail department store - the last of the old style stores. We were going to purchase a dishwasher and a stove. We had a discount coupon - 25% off when you use the store's branded credit card. We selected our appliances and, when checking out, presented our coupon. It turned out the coupon was expired.

We all know that department stores like the one we were in always have some sort of promotion or sale running. In our case, the sales person simply says your coupon is out of date and continues with our sale. I hint that there must be some type of promotion going on.

The sales rep says "nope" and I walk away to leave my wife to finish the sale. Looking around the appliance area, I find a new holiday promotion, for 25% off any purchase, that started the day before. I take a flyer back to the sales person and said, "Is this one out of date also?"

The sales rep had to re-ring up our sale with the new discount.

This was a perfect opportunity for some RA Leadership. If the salesperson had said, "Sir, your coupon is expired but we just started a new promotion that I would gladly apply to your purchase today," then this salesperson would have had a fan for life. I would have been pleasantly shocked.

Instead, there is no way I am going to buy another appliance in that store. Many of you reading this book are going to say that this example is just poor customer service.

But this goes much deeper than simple customer service:

· What was it about this salesperson that prevented him from doing what was obviously right in the first place (providing a current coupon to the customer) without being told to do so by the customer?

· Was the salesperson poorly trained?

· Did the salesperson not care enough?

· Did the salesperson not know about the

current coupon?

· What was it about this salesperson? Was he/she having a bad day?

This salesperson lacked self leadership - the ability to lead oneself to desirable results - in this case a sale and a happy customer. Self leadership is a component of RA Leadership. Remember RA Leadership is leadership that is Inside and Outside, Left and Right, Top and Bottom. Inside and Outside are the self-leadership components of RA Leadership.

This store is a giant retail organization that spends millions of dollars on team member training. It has a team of store managers and district managers who work hard to ensure their team members are equipped with the latest sales and promotional knowledge and material.

Yet at the moment of truth - when it was just the salesman and the customer - the team member failed to lead and take charge of the sale and leave the customer (me) with a positive impression of the salesperson and the retail store.

Ask yourself, "What are my moments of truth? Do I fail or do I succeed?"

I really want to know the answers to those last questions. Put this book down right now, and send me an email at royalston@radioactiveleadership.com.

Place in the email subject line: my moments of truth. If you tell me yours, I'll share mine.

My Moments of Truth:

_____

_____

_____

_____

_____

Police and Fire

Being a Police Officer or a Fire Fighter is a tough vocation. It takes a special sort of person to choose these career paths and it's a pretty certain bet no one out there would say these jobs are easy. These are people who are driven by a sense of purpose and pride - driven by more than money and status.

It's also true that Police Officers and Fire Fighters are like the rest of us - hardworking people who have an important job to do.

Imagine for a moment that you are a police officer working in a large city. You have been on the job now for about 15 years. Some have been good years and others not so good. In our case, the last few years have been challenging, to say the least:

· There was an ugly battle between city council and the police department over raises for officers.

· The city council turned down raises for police officers so the police department took the issue to the citizens.

· In a city wide vote, the citizens voted down a raise for police officers. Your department is now one of the lowest paid in the state in one of the biggest cities in the state.

The anxiety continued: healthcare cost increases with no raise in coverage, police vehicles forced into extended use, low morale throughout the force and a feeling of rejection and apathy from citizens. Some officers consider doing only the bare minimum of service: answer the calls and nothing else.

As you ride along, finishing up a night shift - in a vehicle that is rattling from overuse - you notice a pedestrian has fallen to the ground. As the person's head bounces on the pavement, his buddies reach for him and scream for help. You don't know the situation but you have a decision to make.

What do you do?
>   a) pretend like you don't see this and continue on
>   b) wait until you receive a call over your radio specifically sending you to the location
>   c) stop immediately and render aid

d) call another police officer on the radio to see if they can go by the location

The answer is obviously c).

But this problem illustrates an important point. Our work dynamics, our perceptions of responsibility, change when we rationalize negative feelings. We provide permission to ourselves to do an inadequate job. We allow ourselves to slacken our efforts and damage our results. The logic goes something like this: "I'll show them just how little work I can do, that will teach them!"

Pause for a moment to consider this issue: the person who may show up to save your life is pouting because of an "injustice" at work.

Fortunately for us, the vast majority of Fire Fighters, Police Officers, Paramedics, Doctors, Nurses and other emergency personnel are made of tougher and better stuff.

Which leads us to the next scenario:

All You Can Eat

I live to eat in those "all you can eat" buffet restaurants. You know the ones: Ryan's and Golden Corral. (The names may be different in your area, but the places are similar - more food than imaginable.)

Working in one of these places on a Friday night is a nightmare. Imagine for a moment you are working in one during the dinner rush.

Tables have to be bussed, kids are running around and every(darn)body needs their drinks refilled. You haven't seen even one tip all night. And oh, by the way, several of your fellow employees have called in so you have to do double duty.

Just before your shift, your supervisor tells everyone to make an effort to keep kids unaccompanied by their parents away from the serving lines. Not a problem, right?

Well, you've had to send five kids back to their tables in the last half hour.

You are tired, frustrated, and have only

ten minutes left on your shift. You look up from cleaning a table to see yet another child in line without an adult. This child is making a huge mess. You see one of your co-workers walk right past the unaccompanied child at the serving lines.

What do you do?

Okay, we want to see YOUR answers for this scenario. Fill in 3 non-radioactive responses and one radioactive response.

a) _____

b) _____

c) _____

d) _____

Email me your responses at royalston@radioactiveleadership.com and I will send you mine.

Delivery - Part One

One of the toughest jobs in America has to be an appliance delivery person.

The steps are simple:
· Find the location on an incomprehensible map
· Load the dishwasher
· Get lost because of wrong maps and streets under construction
· Ring to find no one home
· Come back in an hour
· The customer tells you the dishwasher is too   big, wrong color and not the brand they bought
· You call in to find out it's exactly what they ordered
· They remember now
· The water connection is on the wrong side
· You have to charge the customer an extra fee to connect the extension
· The customer tells you to forget it and take it back

What do you do?

    a) pack up and go

    b) call your supervisor

    c) plead with the customer

    d) make rude remarks to the customer

    e) smile and extend the water line to com
       plete the installation

No matter how much we might want to answer d), the correct answer is e). But you already knew that, didn't you? The secret here is no secret at all: your job is to make it work. If you can make the job work, you're supposed to make the job work. So go ahead and get it done.

The Delivery Part Two

Now let's imagine you work in a factory that makes pet products. You know: dog vitamins, pet shampoo, poodle collars, etc. This is a company with a narrow but strong niche, with only one customer - Wal-Mart. (Hey, if you're going to have a single customer, this is the one to have.) This single customer accounts for $20 million per year in revenue - solid and steady revenue.

Our little pet products company employs 150 people; most team members are long term employees - but recently, they've added a bunch of new folks. They're great people, but new and some of them may not have the same work ethic you're used to.

Now Wal-Mart demands products be shipped and delivered on time - NO EXCUSES OR YOU WILL BE DROPPED AS A WAL-MART VENDOR! (It's a subtle strategy, but effective.) In other words, the doors of the small pet products company will close if the Wal-Mart account goes away.

You work in shipping and receiving and there is a very large shipment going out later tonight.   The thing is - it's time for you to go home; you're shift is over. A new guy is responsible getting the shipment out and well, he seems reliable, but you're not sure.

What do you do?

   a) It's not your responsibility - head on home

   b) Intimidate the new guy

   c) Tell a supervisor your concerns

   d) Call back later and offer any help the new guy might need

   e) Stay and make sure the shipment gets out on time

These answers are getting easier, aren't they? It's pretty clear you want to go with d) and/or e) - with my preference being e). Your selection is always based on what you can do to make things work. If it's in your power to help, you must help - no ifs, ands or buts about it. If you can do it, you must do it - it's that simple. Got it?

I feel compelled to address two very important concepts here that you may have a question about - the value of competence and the importance of talent.

The Value of Competence

Your peers will judge you on two measures:

1. Do you say what you mean?
2. Do you do what you say?

Your responsibility is to be sincere with your desires, intentions and actions and then to put those elements to work toward positive results for you and those around you.

While some people dream big dreams, they don't always spend the time and effort to bring those dreams to life. They work on everything except the basics that will deliver actual results. They look toward wishes instead of working on the practical matters what will make those wishes come true. The first step in that process is competence.

Your ability to execute the functions around you is the standard by which others will work. If you radiate competence, full command of your skills, your peers and even your superiors will ramp up their skills to match. Like a basketball player who is always refining his skills, his teammates will also work to keep pace with the player. As personal and team skills increase, the entire team becomes better.

A good player makes a good team better. A great player makes everyone better. More importantly, great players aren't born - they are made through thousands of hours of practice. They master their trade with every device at their command. Their talent seems natural because they've fully mastered their personal competence.

The Importance of Talent

RadioActive Leaders define talent as the **_acquired_** _ability to do something well -_ **_and_** _the continuous enhancement of that ability._ This idea challenges the old adage that talent is a "natural" gift that a person can simply rely upon to achieve their goals. In rare cases that concept may be true - but those cases are rare indeed.

A prime law of RadioActive Leadership is that personal achievement and advancement are completely within the grasp of the RA Leader. There is no outside force or unseen commodity that inhibits their progress or stifles their ability. RA Leaders *own their future* because they determine it themselves. They develop their talents by learning, practicing, applying and refining their abilities. RA Leaders start from where they are, acknowledging challenges and obstacles - working to overcome them. They enhance their strengths and improve on weaknesses.

Most important: RadioActive Leaders own their own future! They don't wait for something to happen to them; they make things happen for themselves.

For many people, this simple concept poses many subtle challenges. Some of us have become quite used to giving up our future to people, actions or incidents beyond our control. Some of this delayed action syndrome may sound familiar:

·I'm waiting for that promotion. They owe it to me.

·They never listen to my ideas. Why should I bother?

·This is the way it's always been done.

·I never have any great ideas. I'm not creative.

·My supervisor doesn't know anything. I just stay out of the way.

·Why should I help the new guy? I don't get paid for that.

·You need a degree to get anywhere. I don't have time to go back to school.

·I'm uncomfortable talking in front of people. I don't want to bring attention to myself.

·Training for the new system is stupid. They'll go back to the old one before we learn it.

There are many ways to rationalize behaviors that limit ability - the list of negative positions is virtually infinite. Even great leaders can fall into subtle traps occasionally - reverting to periods of confusion or immobility. But they

also recognize the symptoms and work to refo-
cus on the possibilities directly in front of them
- they begin with the tools they already have,
not waiting for someone to motivate them or
tell them what to do.

You are in command of your own destiny. No one controls it but you. The degree to
which you succeed is entirely within your own
control.

The Possibility of Failure

"The optimist sees opportunity in every danger. The pessimist sees danger in every opportunity."
                    - Winston Churchill

RA Leaders fail. They understand that failure is an integral element of future success. RA Leaders believe it is much better to act to improve their world than to not act at all - even if some of those actions end in failure. RA Leaders aren't afraid of failure - they understand its inevitability and, while they work to achieve success, they also commit themselves to learn from failure.

RadioActive Leadership is not a guarantee against letdowns or mistakes. Great leaders will take risks and sometimes these risks don't pay off. They review issues, check actions and information - they file each failure as a valuable lesson and then they move on. RA Leaders learn from their mistakes and they turn toward new challenges, adding the experience to their bank of knowledge.

Consider that great basketball player once again, endowed with speed, coordination and jumping ability. These abilities must still be refined through years of repetitive challenges and goals: dribbling techniques, outside shooting, inside drives and much more. Even the greatest players, especially the greatest players, continue to add options to their repertoire in order to overcome new defensive strategies. The refinement of personal skill, and the resultant increased contributions to the team, continues over the career of the great athlete.

The great player doesn't worry over the missed shot or bad pass - the great player gets the ball and shoots or passes again. They imprint the mistake for reference, check for accuracy and consistency and then get right back to work.

And the really great players NEVER stop risking and failing - and then risking more and succeeding more often. They truly great ones don't slow their progress when they've attained a level of achievement. Quite the opposite, the great players increase their dedication and multiply their efforts in order to exceed their own limitations. They work harder on their shot, perfecting the pass and understanding the teammates around them. They seek a level of competence that becomes excellence - where normal to them is untouchable to anyone else. Great leaders embrace the pursuit of perfection. While some people consider perfection unattainable - great leaders seek a success that others assume is impossible.

The Least You Can Do

Competence is the least you owe yourself and your team. Your ability to execute necessary, even ordinary tasks with complete capability is essential to your leadership development. Imagine that you need emergency surgery - (nothing too serious, but you have to go in right now). In an emergency, you won't have the luxury of considering the surgical team's qualifications. You don't have the time or ability to ponder their abilities or talents; you don't know if they were at the front of their class or not. You're wheeled in and the fun must begin.

You do, however, have the right to expect the surgical team is competent. Based on the necessary education and certification, an emergency surgical team will be a group of committed, talented medical professionals - the very least you should expect is competence and commitment.

How does your team perceive you? How do you view yourself? Are you fully competent? Do you know everything that you need to know - do you know everything that you can know about your area of expertise? Your level of specific competence is not merely an indicator of your abilities, it also is directly relevant to your ability to lead. Teammates trust a leader who can not only tell them how to get the job done, but can also do the job itself. Leaders with a complete grasp of the task inspire confidence in their teammates. And a leader who can not only accomplish the task, but also demonstrates excellence in action, inspires individuals to meet or exceed the leader's results.

In order to request results from associates, you must be fully able to demonstrate your ability to achieve those results as well. There can be no barrier you permit for yourself that you don't permit for others - there can be no challenge you delegate that you aren't willing to tackle yourself.

This doesn't mean that you, our Radio-Active Leader, must be successful at every endeavor you attempt - quite the opposite. Leaders must take risks and sometimes fail, just like the rest of us humans. But you must be willing to lead from the middle or the front of the line, in addition to the back areas.

One of the first actions Ross Perot took when he joined the board of General Motors was to get down on the factory floor. He worked alongside some of the auto assembly personnel, had lunch with them, talked about what worked and what didn't. While this was an excellent public relations tactic, it also served the actual purpose of digging up useful, vital information. Perot needed to know what was going on - on the front lines - and he wasn't shy about getting the information. He's a good example of a leader who cuts through the bull to get at what needs to be done.

The concept of complete competence doesn't mean that you have every answer at your fingertips - that is not always possible, nor is it necessary. Great leaders may not have every answer, but they do know how to get the answers they need and how to get them quickly.

Communication

First rule of leadership competence is excellent communication - you must become an expert in conveying your position and relating needs and ideas. You must welcome the challenges of sharing yourself with your peers and team members - as we've seen - this quality assumes risk at your side. You have to put yourself out there, to get others to follow.

There's also an element of diplomacy to the concept of effective communication. In order to make your ideas interesting and attractive, they must be offered in ways that are positive, beneficial and inclusive. It is possible to be assertive with ideas - but that assertion can never take the form of a command.

It's helpful to have your group establish guidelines for ideas and contributions: a set of rules everyone discusses and agrees on, in order to open a free exchange and flow of useful suggestions.

Some general rules:

a) All ideas are good ideas

When brainstorming, or even just chatting, establish the rule that "judgment will be suspended" so that people feel free to offer ideas. There's an important rule that creativity (the formation of something new) and judgment (the review of creative results to determine usefulness) cannot exist at the same time. That is, creativity must be allowed to exist before people judge it.

The activities of creation and judgment are separate entities that must be given their own time and space. In business, judgment kills the creative process before it even begins.

RA Leaders separate the two processes: brainstorming and idea generation occur freely, in their own time frames. Then the judgment process is begun to analyze the results. Most important: the two processes MUST NOT HAPPEN AT THE SAME TIME. Train your people away from saying things like, "I don't like that idea..." or "That would never work." Establish ground rules where everyone considers every idea fully, tossing the ideas around, adding more concepts as you go.

There's a natural evolution to brainstorming: ideas evolve and mutate, conceptions change direction and intention. These circumstances are fine, acceptable in any creative process. What is unacceptable is slaughtering the idea before it has been fully explored.

This takes some tact on your part - you must embody the practice of openness and willingness to risk, before others will follow your example. The results will be startling, though, once your team finds functional directions to explore.

Risk-taking goes up; ideas are offered more freely; the volume of good ideas increases and suddenly, good ideas become reality. This is the way of team creativity - it is the way of true inspiration.

b) Ideas come from agreement, not argument

Move ideas forward by embracing them with passionate acceptance. Encourage your teammates to treat each new idea as a gift to the group, a golden opportunity for everyone involved. This concept is more difficult than it seems. Many people are suspicious of new ideas or set in their ways of working. You can be the catalyst for great ideas by setting the example, embracing each new thought as a great opportunity.

c) Invest time and space on ideas

Most people assume ideas are like lightning bolts - they hit you randomly, out of the clear blue. RA Leaders know that ideas are more like seeds - by caring for them, spending time and effort and cultivating them, you grow more and more.

Delegation

The second rule of leadership competence is delegation - identifying group and task needs and assigning the research and activities required to accomplish the goal. Delegating responsibilities is a key attribute for every good leader - delegation is the second most important quality an RA Leader must enhance.

Many RA Leaders will not possess the public authority that most managers employ to delegate jobs. RA Leaders are peers, not bosses. And while RA Leaders recognize they may not have institutional authority over their peers, RA Leaders achieve other kinds of authority that make them natural leaders: mastery of their craft, understanding of job needs, vision to solve problems, accessibility and openness toward their colleagues. RA Leaders become natural leaders.

Notice that I didn't say, "RA Leaders are born leaders." I didn't use that phrase because it's a myth. Great leaders are not born to leadership; they choose it as a profession, a calling, even a destiny. RA Leaders learn to understand leadership; they grow to embrace it - leadership becomes part of their nature because they immerse themselves in it, making it an extension of their personality, an innate quality of their personality.

This natural appearance can be misleading. Leaders study their calling - they learn important lessons from other leaders. And they learn important lessons from the people around them. As we've seen in other chapters, great leaders and great learners are one and the same.

Negative Positions in Leadership

Here's an interesting tack for you: Radio-Active Leaders spend very little energy on unconstructive conditions in business - other than removing them wherever possible. RA Leaders don't waste time on the typical menu of poor management techniques: assignment of blame, bickering, complaining, gossip and other pettiness. RA Leaders keep their eyes on the prize: positive productivity - and stimulating group efforts to achieve great results. RA Leaders analyze their own practices in order to eradicate poor habits - they scrutinize their behavior to make certain it achieves productive ends.

Sometimes it means they must modify or give up various kinds of behavior.

Here's a list of items RA Leaders give up:

Blame

RA Leaders never search for the scape-goat - they know that the blame game is time-consuming, bad for morale and typically ineffective. They identify people in order to examine responsibility, but they don't worry about finding out "who's fault it is." They analyze the system and results with the entire group and they work toward better production.

Anger

Rage is an entirely useless emotion in business - it doesn't produce positive results for anyone.

Fear

RA Leaders never seek to force fear on their teammates - in fact, usually the opposite is true. There's plenty of fear already present in business - the results of poor production should

167

inspire sufficient fear in any reasonably intelligent human. If you don't get the job done, you won't have the job to do - it's as simple as that.

Selfishness

Leaders become great when their teams do great things. Placing yourself ahead of the team, placing your needs ahead of one or all of your associates, leads to steady decline in effectiveness.

Insecurity

Leaders work to "improve and remove." They improve the qualities needed to increase their ability to lead effectively. And they remove traits that inhibit their capacity to lead and succeed.

Pessimism

Excellent results are a product of accurate goals, affirmative vision, coordinated process and applied effort. In order to define the goals and share the vision, leaders must create the expectation of possible achievement - they must firmly believe they can get the job done and get it done with superior results. Pessimism contradicts vision - it inhibits freedom of expression and the potential for achievement. Constructive analysis is always permissible and desirable - pessimism is not.

It almost sounds too simple - leaders must be positive - but it's true. If you want long-term effectiveness, you will get it faster and more efficiently if you can attract and maintain quality teammates around you. Part of the ability to attract these people resides in your personal character: are you the kind of person other people want to be around?

Generally speaking, few people in business desire the company of a critic or a skeptic. They certainly don't want to be around the downer or pessimist. And all of us run away from the complainers, whiners and cranky types in business. We've all had to spend time with these lovely people and we couldn't get away fast enough.

The development of a positive personality begins in agreement. You agree with who you are, where you are and what you're doing. You eliminate thoughts of resentment or frustration. You put the emotional baggage away - it's not making you any money. Then you begin to agree with your circumstances and situation - this is where I am; this is what I'm doing. This is what I do for a living.

You don't waste time wishing you weren't where you are - you accept it. (For now.) You accept it because, in that acceptance, you begin the process of improving your situation - I'll start from where I am. You don't wait for the next promotion, or until you get back into school, or any other excuse. You don't look at someone else's circumstances and say, "I'm as good as they are. I should have what they have." You are where you are - you must begin here and now.

The conceptual theory of improvement has to begin in the present, not in the future. In a sense, there is no future! Today is the only day I can change - this moment is the only moment that means anything. If I begin here and now, I can change myself and my world. If I wait for something else to happen, anything else to happen, I give my power to something I can't control. As soon as I do that, I give up my future.

We don't want to get melodramatic about this subject - it's one of the more delicate issues in leadership - but it's also important for you to understand. You have to know the effect your behavior and personality has on other people. If you're a drag to be around, people won't want to be around you. And there's nothing that kills motivation quicker than a complainer, whiner or son-of-a-b#$%. Anger, for example, may stimulate short-term results, but long-term, anger kills teams.

More importantly, inappropriate anger plainly demonstrates a lack of personal discipline and responsibility. (Notice we said - inappropriate anger. There are levels of appropriate anger but more about this subject later.) Anger, especially vicious and spontaneous anger, demonstrates a personal loss of control - a subconscious recognition of one's own failure combined with the insecurity to acknowledge or recognize one's own failings. People who rage or explode fail to ultimately understand that they, themselves, have failed - either in planning or execution. Truly abusive people actually understand that they have personally failed, but choose to blame other people anyway.

As a team member, it's good to know the causes and cures of inappropriate anger - you will better understand how to control your own and manage other people's irritation and wrath as well. Leaders learn how to cope with emotional outbursts of all sorts - leaders become adept at managing these circumstances. It's important for you to study the causes, effects and techniques to manage the problems.

Bosses that "blow up" or "fly off the handle" had better also be the owners of the business because, otherwise, they're not going to be around for long. And owners who vent their anger on employees better hope they have a long line of applicants because they won't keep their people - or at any rate, they won't keep their best people.

Yes, there is that odd business philosophy that some bosses show: it's my way or the highway and there's plenty more like you out there. These dinosaurs are dying off like the Edsel or the XFL. They try to achieve positions of power specifically so they can foist their insecurities on people around them. The business world has less and less patience for these types. Productivity is essential for today and the future - misdirected anger is counterproductive so these clowns are moved out. If you currently work for one of these old boys, check around for other options - you don't want to be caught in their downward spiral.

We've dealt with inappropriate or misdirected anger - these are negative expressions of a person's inability to manage their needs. There are times and places that call for appropriate intense emotion. For example, let's say you have a valuable team associate that, for some reason, just can't seem to show up to work on time. You've explored causes and resolutions; you've coached this person on proper participation and behavior. You've been clear that their failure to arrive on time causes problems beyond their personal needs or productivity. Yet still, the problem persists.

It's appropriate to tell this person you are angry about their inability to control their own conduct or circumstances. You've thought about it and worked toward resolving the problem - yet the problem does not go away. It's fully acceptable to show irritation and frustration at the lack of progress - it's a normal and very human expression.

First though, you've shown the chronically late person, and your team associates, that you've explored many avenues of expression: identifying the problem and its effects, working toward a reasonable and agreed solution, creating an atmosphere of open communication and participation. After you've taken these steps, and progress is not shown, its quite normal to be frustrated. And it's also normal to let people know your frustration - as long as your intention is still to find resolution to the problem.

Oddly enough, some rare situations can only be resolved through firm or intense emotions - some people only respond when warned forcefully. If they're ultimately productive people, then intense emotion is a useful tool to keep them productive. But anger is not the first emotion you exhibit in these cases, nor is it something you use accidentally or without control. Truly "blowing up" at someone does nothing to resolve the situation - rage only serves the person enraged.

More importantly, rage lowers your level of authority and competence. Associates and subordinates will assume, correctly, that your inability to control yourself is an indication of weakness and lack of discipline. Anger combined with blame shuts down communication in every direction - people run for cover and fingers become pointed in every direction other than the right one. So rage inhibits virtually every vital pathway to communication and cooperation among teammates. It diminishes the ability to lead and damages the possible future of teams and their leaders.

Pessimism is a sneaky crook. It steals momentum through the disguise of authority or experience. Pessimism creeps in, pretending to be the voice of experience; when in reality, it's an excuse not to work.

In the real world, pessimism is useless, a consumer of energy and passion and a waste of time and goodwill. The simple, sometimes trite, fact is - pessimism is a self-fulfilling prediction. If you believe it can't be done, it can't be done. The opposite is also true.

We won't get too deep into inspiration and motivation here - suffice to say that every great achievement in the history of mankind was met with resistance either small or large. Great discoverers, inventors, statesmen, holy people - were all told they would fail, at great cost to themselves. They heard the objections, they suffered the obstructions and they chose to achieve against the odds and in spite of the opposition. Good things happen, small and large, because people decide they can and should happen - and they work toward those good things with devotion and energy. This is the way of useful, enduring productivity - it is the way to be truly valuable to yourself and your world.

Anger is the bully's way of relieving himself of responsibility. Anger is a cop-out, a way to blame someone or something other than the person who's losing his temper. As we outlined earlier, RA Leaders must accept the responsibility for his or her relationships. The same goes with results. An RA Leader accepts the conditions of his own actions. If the job gets done correctly, there's plenty of praise to go around. If the job gets done poorly, or didn't get done at all, raging around doesn't solve the problem - it makes it worse.

Anger also demonstrates a serious inability to control oneself. And when people display anger, when they "lose it" or "throw a fit," they're really showing everyone they can't control themselves. Worse yet, they're showing everyone they don't actually know how to get things done.

We've all had the kind of boss who believes yelling is the only way to get results. We also know that boss was an idiot.

As you grow in your RadioActive Leadership, you'll go much farther showing a stern and open concern about results, rather than blasting people around you.

The Cost of Poor Leadership

"Duty is the sense of obligation which motivates one to do, to the best of his ability, what is expected of him in any assigned position or situation"
- Any USMA Graduate

Business has a few advantages over law enforcement and military vocations. The pay is usually better, the hours are much easier and, in business, when leadership fails, it doesn't usually mean someone is going to die. But for most of us, business relates to security, opportunity, fulfillment and related benefits. This is a bonus because while the fear of imminent death is a very motivating factor, it's also a stressor that most people would prefer to avoid.

Having said that - leadership failure in business doesn't usually mean that people die - leadership failure in business may contribute to the death of companies, businesses and even entire industries. The list of business failures directly linked to leadership problems is virtually infinite - from the family business that failed to consider succession issues to multinational conglomerates that cast away its best minds - leadership failure is key contributor to the death of companies.

As important as the subject of leadership failure is, in the context of business today, poor leadership skills also cost businesses money and time. Lack of direction, non-inclusive decisions, poor communication, consensus failure - each of these elements contribute directly to additional costs in production, execution, delivery and follow-up in literally all areas of the business world. In addition to the initial, day to day costs: duplication of efforts, failed sales, disaffected customers, turmoil in key workplace areas, etc. poor leadership contributes to long-term costs: loss of key personnel, stifled innovation, low-quality production, limited risk-taking (if any) and much more.

Imagine how much money has been spent, in every industry, simply trying to get everyone directed toward specific end goals. The costs are staggering.

Cooperative Leadership

This is where you come in. You can begin where you are right now, today. Unlike people in upper management, who have to wait for the next big meeting to enact their strategy or get their point across, you don't have to wait to begin leading. You can do it now, or tomorrow - whenever you decide to lead well and usefully. You can affect change, save money, find efficiencies, inspire yourself and others - you can share ideas, compare methods, work on solutions, brainstorm, rally and go out for lunch with the gang. All this is within your current power and authority - you don't have to wait for anyone to ask you or wait for anyone to tell you. You can do what you want to do and you can do it now.

This is one of your advantages in being on the front lines - the ability to act now, if you choose to act at all. Another significant advantage is your ability to improve your situation, and your organization's conditions right now and in a way that makes your group noticed and valuable. A point of sale idea that raises revenue in your retail department, a solution to service problems in a restaurant, a more efficient method of coding inventory in your warehouse - each of these ideas will not only increase the efficiency of your organization, they also increase YOUR value in the organization itself.

The Beginning of the Beginning

By now you should be familiar with a fundamental RadioActive Leadership law: It's Up To You. As we wrap up this book and begin emitting the power and energy of RA Leadership, it's vital to restate this life-altering principle: you are in complete control of your present actions and future direction.

There is no outside force or unseen influence that can stop you from moving forward, upward and outward. As your talents can flourish when you provide study, attention and dedication - your limitations can also take hold from lack of effort or surrendering your determination to some outside force.

The people around you can help your future more than you can possibly imagine. Your job is to connect with them so that they can help you while you're helping them. Through RadioActive connections, you progress forward while you help others do the same.

This means you must start today, from where you are right now. There's no waiting for something to happen or somebody to take over for you - you're going to get on your feet and make a phone call to brainstorm with an associate or chat with a friend about future options or meet a coworker to go over dreams, plans and possibilities. It starts now.

There's an old saying: things done for goodness' sake are never wasted. In RA Leadership we interpret that to be: any positive action, even the smallest effort, moves you closer to your ultimate goals. And a thousand small steps move you much farther along than ten giant ones. Don't wait for the giant steps - start with the small ones right now.

Finally, I want to thank you for being part of my personal goals and dreams. This book is one small step for me, on my path of realizing my own RadioActive potential. By connecting with you through this book, I truly hope that you'll bring your own unique strengths and astonishing dreams back to me. As we unite with the other RadioActive Leaders around the world, we will forge visions and ideas into incredible realities. That's one of my goals, one of my RadioActive plans.

So email me your thoughts and plans - and I'll share mine. It's time we get started working on them together.

Roy Alston - RadioActive Leader